THE NEXT CHAPTER
A
CHRISTMAS
CAROL

A Christmas Carol

Copyright © 2024 by Gary J. Rose. All rights reserved.

No part of this publication may be reproduced, stored in a retrieval system, or transmitted in any form or by any means, digital, electronic, mechanical, photocopying, recording, or otherwise, or conveyed via the Internet or a website without prior written permission of the publisher, except in the case of brief quotations embodied in critical articles and reviews.

This is a work of fiction. Names, characters, places, and incidents are products of the author's imagination or have been used fictitiously and are not to be construed as real. Any resemblance to persons, living or dead, actual events, locales, or organizations is coincidental.

ISBN: 979-8-9918839-3-1 (hardback)
             979-8-9918839-2-4 (paperback)

Printed in the United States of America

THE NEXT CHAPTER
A CHRISTMAS CAROL

A Christmas Novella

GARY J. ROSE

Acknowledgement

I want to extend my heartfelt thanks to all my fans—those who have supported my Jeannie Loomis thriller series, my horror novels, and my Christmas novellas: *The Hidden Workshop*, *A Christmas Carousel*, and *Home for the Holidays*. Your feedback on the draft manuscript of *A Christmas Carol: The Next Chapter* and your encouragement to publish it before Christmas 2024 have meant the world to me.

    I sincerely hope you enjoy this continuation of Charles Dickens' classic, *A Christmas Carol*. Your enthusiasm and support keep me inspired to write, and I couldn't have done it without you.

Preface

I cannot recall the very first time I watched any of the numerous *A Christmas Carol* adaptations. One vivid memory, however, involves being at my aunt's house, where total chaos reigned, but amidst all the hustle, the 1951 film *Scrooge*, starring Alastair Sim, was playing on the black-and-white television. The timeless story captivated me, even if it was only a fragment of the film.

Later in life, Christmas wouldn't be the same without revisiting the original 1935 adaptation of *Scrooge*, featuring Seymour Hicks as the old miser. This version ends with Scrooge waking up on Christmas morning, determined to change his ways. It depicts his earnest attempts to embrace generosity and compassion, as he visits Fred, his nephew, to reconnect with family and surprises the Cratchit family with gifts. The ending shows Scrooge as a transformed man, committed to living in the spirit of Christmas.

Then came the aforementioned 1951 *Scrooge*, often regarded as one of the best adaptations of Dickens' story. Alastair Sim's portrayal of Scrooge is iconic, ending with a heartfelt transformation after the Ghosts of Christmas guide him through his past, present, and possible future. Sim's Scrooge wakes up overcome with joy and laughter, embracing the spirit of love and generosity. He surprises Bob Cratchit with a raise and helps his family, and also joins his nephew Fred's family for the Christmas celebrations, highlighting his newfound joy and commitment to helping those around him.

The 1970 musical version starred Albert Finney as Scrooge and Alec Guinness as the Ghost of Marley. After a night filled with visions from the Ghosts of Christmas, Scrooge awakens on Christmas morning, reborn with joy and determination to change his ways. He dances through the streets of London, buys a large turkey for the Cratchit family, forgives debts, and visits his nephew Fred's home to share in the festivities. The film ends with a joyful Christmas dinner, emphasizing Scrooge's complete transformation.

In 1984, one of my all-time favorite actors, George C. Scott, took on the role of Scrooge. In this faithful adaptation, Scott captures the sternness of the character while also portraying his ultimate transformation. The film ends with Scrooge waking up on Christmas morning, filled with newfound joy. He donates to charity, reconciles with his nephew, surprises the Cratchit family with gifts, and raises Bob's salary. Scott's portrayal of Scrooge's transformation feels genuine, and the ending emphasizes his commitment to kindness and generosity, concluding with warmth as he joins Fred's family for the Christmas celebrations.

In 1999, Patrick Stewart took on the role of Scrooge in a made-for-television adaptation of *A Christmas Carol*. This film ends with Scrooge waking up on Christmas morning overwhelmed with gratitude for his second chance at life. He immediately sets out to make things right, buying the Cratchits a turkey and giving Bob a raise. Stewart's Scrooge, like his predecessors, is depicted with a heartfelt desire to change, becoming more caring and compassionate.

Disney also offered an animated adaptation of *A Christmas Carol*, though it strayed considerably from the original text. Yet, like the others, it ends with Scrooge's transformation into a generous and caring man.

The most recent adaptation I recall watching is the 2019 miniseries *A Christmas Carol*, presented by FX/BBC. This version takes a darker approach, emphasizing the haunting elements of Scrooge's journey. He is, once again, visited by the Ghosts of Christmas, and he slowly realizes the extent of his past mistakes. The ending, however, is more somber compared to other versions, suggesting that Scrooge's transformation is gradual and requires ongoing effort. Despite the darker tone, Scrooge is committed to changing his ways.

Each of these adaptations has left an indelible mark on the legacy of *A Christmas Carol*, showcasing the universal appeal of Dickens' timeless tale. But even after all these years of enjoying these various versions, one question has always lingered in my mind: what happened to Ebenezer Scrooge after Christmas Day?

Did his transformation endure, or did the inevitable challenges of life test his resolve? It is this curiosity—this need to explore what lies beyond the jubilant endings—that inspired me to write *A Christmas Carol – The Next Chapter*. Through this novel, I wanted to imagine a continuation of Scrooge's journey, delving deeper into his redemption and exploring the lives he touched along the way.

The original novel by Charles Dickens, published in 1843, spans between 109 and 112 pages, depending on the font and formatting used by various publishing houses. As a tribute to Dickens, I set out to replicate the length of *A*

Christmas Carol – The Next Chapter to mirror that of the original. I am pleased to say that I have accomplished this goal.

It is my dream that, long after I am gone, readers who have either read the original Dickens novel or watched one of the numerous film adaptations will seek out this novel to discover the next chapter in the life of Ebenezer Scrooge. May it serve as a testament to the enduring spirit of redemption, generosity, and the joy that comes from embracing the true meaning of Christmas.

Chapter 1

Snow fell gently on the cobbled streets of Victorian London. The glow of gas lamps cast a golden hue over the scene, illuminating the gentle snowfall. Smoke from chimneys lazily reached for the sky, mingling with the crisp winter air. The shops lining the streets were decorated festively, their windows adorned with wreaths, garlands, and cheerful lights that bathed the street in a warm glow. People bustled to and fro, their laughter and chatter filling the night air, exchanging hearty greetings of "Merry Christmas" as they passed one another.

Ebenezer Scrooge stood at Fred's doorstep, his cheeks rosy from laughter, a smile on his face that seemed foreign but felt natural. Fred, his nephew, and Clara, Fred's wife, stood beside him, both enveloped in the warm glow spilling from the open doorway. The warmth of the light contrasted against the chill of the winter evening, casting long shadows onto the cobbled street.

"Uncle, you have made this Christmas one we will never forget," Fred said, his eyes filled with joy and sincerity. Clara nodded in agreement, her smile softening the night even further.

Ebenezer nodded, his eyes glistening. "And you, dear boy, have reminded me what it truly means to be part of a family. I am so grateful."

Fred smiled warmly, pulling Clara closer to him, his arm wrapped protectively around her shoulders. "Don't be a stranger, Uncle. You'll always have a seat at our table, no matter the occasion," Clara added, her voice sincere and welcoming.

"I'll hold you to that, Clara," Scrooge replied, his smile broadening. "Thank you, my dear. Merry Christmas to you both!" Scrooge tipped his hat, drawing his coat tightly around himself, and took a step back. Fred and Clara stood in the doorway, waving as he descended the steps. The joy and warmth from their home lingered with him as he turned, walking away from the comfort of family back into the cold embrace of London's night.

The city's evening had settled in, and Scrooge walked briskly through the bustling streets, his eyes taking in everything around him as though for the first time. Snow crunched beneath his boots, a sound that, once unnoticed, now seemed delightful. In the distance he could hear carolers singing a Christmas song that he hummed to himself. He nodded and tipped his hat to a passing carriage driver, who returned the gesture with a smile.

"Merry Christmas, madam!" Scrooge called out to a woman passing by, her arms full with a basket of bright red apples. She looked up, startled for a moment, before a smile bloomed across her face. "A good night for apples, madam!" Scrooge called jovially. The woman laughed, her laughter ringing like bells.

"Indeed, sir! Care for one?" she offered, holding up an apple.

"I think I shall," he replied, grabbing an apple and giving her a coin far greater than the asking price.

"Oh, thank you sir. Merry Christmas to you as well!" she replied, her voice kind. Scrooge returned the smile, warmth spreading through his chest as he continued on his way.

As he rounded a corner, he noticed a figure huddled in the shadows of an alleyway. It was a beggar, dressed in tattered clothes, his face barely visible beneath a worn cap. Scrooge paused for a moment, his heart heavy at the sight. He reached into his coat pocket and approached the man, kneeling slightly to be closer to eye level.

"Here you are, my good fellow," Scrooge said, offering the man a silver coin. The beggar's eyes widened, his fingers trembling as he took the coin.

"Bless you, sir," the man murmured, his voice thick with gratitude. He touched the brim of his cap, a gesture of thanks, before glancing down at the coin in disbelief.

"The blessings are yours to keep," Scrooge replied warmly, tilting his hat before standing again. He continued along his way, whistling a cheerful tune, feeling a sense of purpose and joy in his heart that had long been absent.

Further along, the bustling sounds of the city began to fade, replaced by the soft whistle of the wind weaving through the narrow streets. Scrooge smiled as he felt the bite of the crisp winter air on his cheeks, the glow of the streetlamps lighting his path. Ahead, he spotted another carriage driver, and he lifted his hat in greeting.

"Merry Christmas!" he called, his voice ringing out in the stillness of the night.

The driver tipped his hat in return, a smile spreading across his face. Scrooge continued on, turning another corner, when he once again saw the woman with the basket of apples, now standing beneath the glow of a nearby lamppost.

As he made his way home, Scrooge marveled at the sights and sounds of the city. The once cold, indifferent streets now seemed alive with wonder and joy. For the first time in many years, Ebenezer Scrooge felt the true spirit of Christmas—a spirit of love, kindness, and warmth.

Chapter 2

The wind whispered softly as Scrooge made his way down the quieter, darker streets that led to his home. The snow, which had earlier blanketed the bustling city in festive brightness, now seemed to gather in solemn drifts along the cobbled paths. The gas lamps that lined the road flickered, their flames struggling to remain lit, casting long, wavering shadows on the buildings. The glow that had once felt warm now seemed dimmer, as though hesitant to penetrate the growing darkness.

Scrooge's pace slowed. His cheerful whistling faltered, replaced by silence as he took in the street around him. He felt a chill that had nothing to do with the cold air, an uneasy feeling settling in his bones. His eyes darted to the shadows lurking between the houses, and though he saw nothing out of place, his instincts whispered otherwise. He shook his head, a wry smile tugging at his lips. "Nonsense, Ebenezer," he muttered under his breath. "Just shadows and tricks of the light." With a force of will, he brushed away the unease, quickening his steps until he reached his home.

The house loomed before him, an imposing structure made all the more eerie by the pale moonlight. The heavy front door, with its brass knocker, stood before him, silent and still. Scrooge approached, his gaze shifting upwards. And there, for a fleeting moment, he saw it—the brass knocker shimmered, shifting until it took the form of a face. Marley's face.

His breath caught, visible in the cold night air. He stared at the knocker, a thousand memories rushing through his mind in an instant. Marley—his old partner, the man who had once shared in his pursuit of wealth and power, and who had returned to warn him that his life was on the wrong path. The face held no malice now, only a silent watchfulness.

Scrooge drew in a deep breath, letting it out in a puff of misty vapor. "Not tonight, old friend," he said softly, almost affectionately, as though speaking to a beloved ghost. A nervous chuckle escaped his lips, and he shook his head. The knocker shifted back, returning to its original brass state, and Scrooge, with a sigh of relief, pushed the heavy door open.

The door creaked on its hinges, the sound echoing in the stillness of the night. He stepped into the entryway, the chill of the outdoors giving way to the muted warmth of his home. Scrooge closed the door behind him with a gentle thud, the latch clicking softly as it settled. Silence greeted him—comfortable, familiar silence—broken only by the soft crackle of the fire burning in the hearth.

Scrooge removed his hat and coat, hanging them on the wooden hooks by the door. His home, though large and somewhat grand, was sparsely decorated, a reflection of the man he had been for so many years. The furniture was old but well-kept, and the house had an air of both comfort and loneliness. The flickering fire cast long shadows on the walls, the flames dancing and creating shapes that moved with the light.

He moved to a small table that stood near the armchair by the fire. On the table rested a wooden box, its surface polished and worn with age. Scrooge opened the box with careful hands, his expression softening as he took out an old, delicate locket. He held it up, turning it gently until the firelight caught on the small portrait inside. The face of a young woman smiled back at him—his sister, Fan.

"Fan," Scrooge whispered, his voice filled with warmth and regret. "If only you could see me now." His gaze lingered on the portrait, the memory of her laughter filling his mind, a memory untouched by the passing years. She had always believed in him, always seen the good in him, even when he could not. And now, more than ever, he wished she could see the man he was becoming, a man striving to be better, to honor the love she had given him.

A faint smile crossed his lips, and he carefully set the locket down. He turned to the armchair, sinking into it with a contented sigh. The fire crackled softly, its warmth seeping into his bones, easing the tension he hadn't realized he was carrying. He let his eyes drift closed, the exhaustion of the day catching up with him.

The shadows on the wall flickered, dancing in the light of the fire. For a moment, they seemed to shift, the shapes elongating and darkening until they almost formed the outline of a hunched figure. The shadow lingered, its form twisting unnaturally, before fading back into the gentle, flickering light.

Scrooge remained oblivious, his breathing evening out as sleep began to claim him. The warmth of the fire, the softness of the chair, and the quiet of his home lulled him into slumber. Outside, the wind howled softly, the world beyond his door growing colder and darker, but inside, Ebenezer Scrooge rested, a smile still playing on his lips.

Tonight, there would be no ghosts, no visions of what could be or what had been. There would only be peace—the peace of a man who had faced his past and chosen a different future. And as the fire burned low, the shadows settled, and the old house grew quiet once more, Ebenezer Scrooge slept, unaware of the strange and shifting shapes that lingered just beyond the edge of the light.

The door creaked shut behind Scrooge as he stepped into the dimly lit hallway. He hung his coat and hat on a brass hook near the door, glancing at the darkened interior of the house.

"Ah, how quiet you've become," he said with a smile. "And I wouldn't have it any other way."

He lit a small lantern, its warm glow illuminating the modest but tidy space. The faint crackle of the fire in the hearth drew him toward the sitting room. Scrooge set the lantern on the mantelpiece and stirred the embers of the fire, coaxing the flames to life. He retrieved a small cup of tea from the side table and sank into his armchair with a contented sigh. His eyes drifted back to the wooden box on the table beside him. With care, he opened it again, taking out the locket containing the portrait of his sister, Fan.

"Dear Fan, I've finally done it," he said softly. He smiled wistfully, then closed the locket and set it beside the box. The firelight flickered, casting shadows on the walls. Scrooge's gaze lingered on the shifting shapes, his expression briefly clouding with unease.

A distant sound—like the faint clinking of chains—echoed faintly. Scrooge stiffened, looking toward the hallway. "Bah... my imagination playing tricks," he muttered, shaking his head and turning back to the fire, settling deeper into the chair.

Chapter 3

Scrooge awoke to the pale light of early morning filtering through the curtains of his sitting room. He blinked groggily, the warmth of the hearth having lulled him into a deep sleep the night before. Slowly, he sat up in his armchair, feeling the stiffness in his back from spending the night there. The fire had burned down to a faint glow of embers, the room chilly now as the morning air seeped in through the windows.

With a sigh, Scrooge stood, stretching his limbs as he glanced around the familiar room. The locket of his sister, Fan, still rested on the side table, and he reached over to pick it up once more. He turned it over in his hand, staring at her portrait as memories of his sister filled his mind.

"Dear Fan," he whispered. "Perhaps today, I'll do something you would be proud of."

Setting the locket back in the box, Scrooge straightened his coat and made his way to the kitchen. The house was silent, the only sounds those of his footsteps echoing across the wooden floors. He busied himself with making a modest breakfast—a piece of bread toasted over the fire, a cup of tea brewed in an old iron kettle. As he ate, he looked out the small kitchen window, watching as the sun slowly rose over the rooftops of London.

The city was waking up. He could see people moving about, bundled in coats and scarves as they hurried along the cobbled streets. Children ran past, their laughter echoing faintly through the glass, and Scrooge couldn't help but smile. It was the day after Christmas, and for the first time in many years, he felt the lingering joy of the holiday.

After finishing his meal, Scrooge decided he could no longer stay cooped up in his home. There was a world out there, and he intended to be a part of it. He donned his coat and hat, wrapping a scarf snugly around his neck before stepping out into the crisp morning air. The chill hit him immediately, but it was invigorating, waking him fully as he closed the door behind him and made his way down the steps to the street.

The streets of London were bustling with activity. The market stalls were open, their vendors calling out cheerfully to passersby, offering everything from fresh produce to handmade trinkets. Scrooge walked slowly, taking in the sights and sounds around him. He greeted those he passed, his heart warming at the smiles and greetings he received in return. It was a far cry from the days when people would avoid meeting his eye, when his reputation as a miser had kept others at a distance.

As he walked, Scrooge found himself drawn to a small group gathered near a street corner. They were carolers, singing a lively rendition of "God Rest Ye Merry, Gentlemen." Their voices were rich and full, harmonizing beautifully as they sang. Scrooge paused, listening with a smile on his face. He reached into his coat pocket and pulled out a coin, dropping it into the collection box they had set out.

"Merry Christmas to you all," he said, his voice loud enough to be heard over the singing.

The carolers beamed at him, their song continuing without missing a beat. Scrooge nodded to them, his heart light as he continued on his way. He walked without a destination in mind, simply enjoying the morning and the company of the people around him.

As he moved through the streets, Scrooge began to notice the little things—the shopkeepers sweeping their steps, the children playing with their new toys, the mothers carrying baskets filled with goods. He felt a deep sense of connection to the people around him, as though he were seeing them truly for the first time.

Eventually, Scrooge found himself in front of a small bakery. The scent of fresh bread wafted out into the street, making his stomach rumble. He stepped inside, the bell above the door chiming softly as he entered. The baker, a plump woman with rosy cheeks, looked up from behind the counter and smiled.

"Good morning, sir! What can I get for you today?" she asked.

Scrooge returned her smile, his eyes glancing over the rows of bread and pastries. "Good morning! I think I'll take a loaf of your finest bread," he replied, reaching into his pocket.

The baker wrapped the loaf in brown paper, handing it to him with a nod. "That'll be three pence, sir."

Scrooge placed the coins on the counter, then hesitated for a moment. He looked at the baker, his expression softening. "You know, I think

I'll take another loaf as well. And if you could, perhaps give it to someone who might need it?"

The baker's eyes widened in surprise, and she smiled warmly. "Of course, sir. That's very kind of you."

Scrooge nodded, taking his loaf and tucking it under his arm. "Thank you. And a very Merry Christmas to you."

"Merry Christmas to you as well, sir," the baker replied, her voice filled with genuine gratitude.

Scrooge left the bakery, his heart feeling lighter with each step he took. He walked through the streets, stopping now and then to greet people, to share a kind word or a smile. He even bought a few small toys from a street vendor, handing them out to children who looked as though they could use a bit of cheer.

As the day wore on, Scrooge found himself near a familiar building—the orphanage he had passed so many times before, always too absorbed in his own affairs to take notice. Today, though, he paused, looking up at the modest structure. The windows were decorated with simple wreaths, and he could hear the faint sound of children's laughter from within.

Without a second thought, Scrooge made his way up the steps and knocked on the door. After a moment, a woman in her middle years opened it, her expression curious. "Good afternoon, sir. How can I help you?"

"Good afternoon," Scrooge replied, his voice gentle. "I was wondering if there might be something I could do to help today. Perhaps a donation, or... well, anything at all."

The woman's eyes softened, and she stepped aside, gesturing for him to enter. "That's very generous of you, sir. Please, come in."

Scrooge stepped inside, the warmth of the orphanage wrapping around him like a comforting blanket. He could see children playing in the main room, their laughter filling the space. The woman led him to a small office, where she introduced herself as Mrs. Hayworth, the head of the orphanage.

"We do our best to provide for the children, but any help is always appreciated," Mrs. Hayworth said, her voice tinged with weariness. Scrooge nodded, his heart going out to her and the children under her care.

"Please, Mrs. Hayworth, take this," Scrooge said, reaching into his coat and pulling out his coin pouch. He handed it to her, the weight of the coins clinking softly as she accepted it. "Use it for whatever you need—for food, clothing, anything that will make their lives a bit brighter."

Mrs. Hayworth's eyes glistened with unshed tears, and she smiled. "Thank you, sir. You have no idea what this means to us."

Scrooge shook his head, his own eyes misting. "It's the least I can do. I've spent too many years focused only on myself. It's time I started giving back."

Mrs. Hayworth nodded, her smile growing. "Would you like to stay for a while? The children would love to meet you."

Scrooge hesitated for only a moment before nodding. "I'd be honored."

Mrs. Hayworth led him into the main room, where the children looked up, their eyes wide with curiosity. Scrooge smiled at them, his heart swelling with a warmth he hadn't felt in years.

"Hello, children," he said, his voice gentle. "I'm Mr. Scrooge. I thought I'd come by and see if I could bring a bit of Christmas cheer."

The children gathered around, their laughter and excitement filling the room as they introduced themselves. Scrooge spent the afternoon with them, telling stories, listening to their dreams, and even joining in a game or two. The joy on their faces was more rewarding than any profit he had ever made, and as the sun began to set, Scrooge knew that this was where he was meant to be—among people, sharing in their lives, and making a difference.

As he left the orphanage, Mrs. Hayworth saw him to the door, her gratitude evident in her eyes. "Thank you again, Mr. Scrooge. You've made this day truly special."

Scrooge nodded, his own heart full. "And you, Mrs. Hayworth, have reminded me of what truly matters. Merry Christmas to you all."

"Merry Christmas, Mr. Scrooge," she replied, waving as he made his way down the steps.

The sky was painted in hues of orange and pink as the day gave way to evening. Scrooge walked home, his heart lighter than it had ever been. He had spent so many years in darkness, but now, he could see the light—and he intended to follow it, wherever it led.

CHAPTER 4

The day after Boxing Day dawned with a crisp chill that lingered in the air, and Ebenezer Scrooge was determined to continue his journey of transformation. He stepped out of his front door, pulling his coat tightly around him, the cold biting at his cheeks. The streets of London were already busy with activity, but as Scrooge made his way into town, he noticed something peculiar.

The shopkeepers and townspeople, who had greeted each other with warmth and friendliness, seemed to falter when they caught sight of him. There were hesitant glances, awkward smiles that quickly faded, and even the occasional hurried step to avoid crossing his path. Scrooge could see them whispering to each other, their eyes darting his way, uncertainty written across their faces.

Scrooge paused at the window of a small shop, glancing at his reflection. He looked different—lighter, softer somehow—but it was clear that many still saw him as the man he had been only days ago. The miserly, cold-hearted businessman who had cared for nothing but his wealth. He sighed, a pang of regret hitting him. He had caused a great deal of harm to the people in this community and earning back their trust would take time.

As he continued on, he approached a familiar greengrocer's stall, the scent of fresh produce filling the crisp air. The greengrocer, a middle-aged man with a thick mustache, looked up, his eyes widening as Scrooge approached. He shifted uneasily, his hand resting protectively over the apples displayed in front of him.

"Good morning, Mr. Thompson," Scrooge called, his voice warm and genuine. He reached into his coat pocket and pulled out a few coins. "A fine morning for fresh apples, wouldn't you say?"

Thompson blinked, his expression one of surprise. "Uh, yes, Mr. Scrooge, I suppose it is," he stammered, glancing at the coins Scrooge held out.

Scrooge placed the coins on the counter, taking an apple in return. "You know, I've always admired the quality of your produce," he said with a smile. "And I must apologize if I've ever been... less than neighborly."

Thompson hesitated, his eyes searching Scrooge's face as if trying to determine whether he was sincere. Slowly, he nodded, a tentative smile touching his lips. "Thank you, Mr. Scrooge. That's very kind of you."

Scrooge tipped his hat, the apple in hand. "Merry Christmas, Mr. Thompson. And all the best for the new year."

"M-Merry Christmas to you as well, sir," Thompson replied, still looking bewildered as Scrooge walked away, whistling softly to himself.

Scrooge continued down the street, the apple's crisp sweetness a reminder of the simple pleasures he had once ignored. As he rounded a corner, he caught sight of a pair of children, their noses pressed against the window of a toy shop. They stared longingly at the display of wooden trains and dolls, their eyes filled with wonder. Scrooge paused, watching them for a moment before stepping closer.

"Beautiful toys, aren't they?" he said, his voice gentle. The children looked up, startled, their eyes wide as they recognized him. They nodded, but took a cautious step back, considering running away from the miser who had chased them a few days earlier while singing carols.

Scrooge's heart sank at their reaction, but he knelt down to their level, his gaze soft. "Tell me, do you have any toys like these at home?"

The little girl shook her head, her brother remaining silent. Scrooge smiled, standing and reaching into his pocket. He entered the toy shop, the bell above the door jingling as he pushed it open. The shopkeeper looked up, startled, his eyes narrowing slightly at the sight of Scrooge.

"Good day, Mr. Scrooge," the shopkeeper said cautiously.

"Good day indeed," Scrooge replied, his tone bright. "I'd like to purchase a few toys for those children outside, if you don't mind. Something special for each of them."

The shopkeeper's eyes widened in surprise, and after a moment, he nodded. "Of course, sir. I'll see to it right away."

Scrooge selected a small wooden train and a beautiful doll, both carefully crafted, and handed them to the shopkeeper. He paid for them without hesitation, then turned and walked back outside, the toys held carefully in his hands.

He approached the children once more, kneeling down again. "These are for you," he said, holding out the gifts. "Consider them a late Christmas present."

The children stared at the toys, then at Scrooge, their expressions slowly transforming from fear to disbelief, and finally to joy. The little girl took the doll, her eyes wide, while her brother gingerly accepted the train.

"Thank you, sir," the boy whispered, his voice barely audible. "And Merry Christmas to you too."

Scrooge smiled, his eyes misting. "You're very welcome. And remember, Christmas is a time for joy and kindness. Cherish it, my young friends."

The children beamed, their faces lighting up as they clutched their new treasures. They turned and ran off, their laughter ringing out as they disappeared down the street. Scrooge watched them go, his heart swelling with a warmth he hadn't known in years.

Scrooge continued his walk, his thoughts turning once more to Marley. He could almost feel Marley's presence beside him, as if his old partner were watching over him, a silent witness to his transformation. The memory of Marley's visit—his ghostly face, the chains that bound him—was still vivid in Scrooge's mind. He knew that Marley had suffered greatly in death because of the choices he had made in life, choices not unlike Scrooge's own.

Scrooge paused in front of a bench, the chill of the wind biting at his skin. He sat down, looking out over the bustling street, the people moving past without a second glance. He thought of Marley, of the chains forged in life, each link a testament to greed and missed opportunities for kindness. Scrooge shivered, not from the cold, but from the weight of understanding.

"Jacob, old friend," he whispered, his voice barely audible above the noise of the street. "I hope you can see me now. I hope you know that I've changed, and that your warning wasn't in vain."

He closed his eyes for a moment, the sounds of the city fading as he allowed himself to remember. He remembered Marley's face, twisted in regret, and he remembered the spirits that had visited him—the past, the present, and the future all laid bare before him, showing him the man he had been and the man he could become. He had been given a second chance, and he would not waste it.

Scrooge opened his eyes, a determined smile spreading across his face. He stood, brushing the snow from his coat as he resumed his walk. He had much to do—much to make amends for, and many lives to touch. He would continue to spread kindness, to be a part of the world rather than apart from it.

As he made his way down the street, Scrooge considered his next steps. He thought of Bob Cratchit and his son, who were likely at the office today, working diligently. He had promised a brighter future for them, and he intended to keep that promise.

Scrooge quickened his pace, heading toward his counting house. When he arrived, he paused for a moment outside the door, listening to the sounds within—the scratching of a quill, the faint murmur of conversation. He smiled, pushing the door open and stepping inside.

Bob Cratchit looked up from his desk, his eyes widening in surprise. "Mr. Scrooge! Good morning, sir."

"Good morning, Bob!" Scrooge replied, his voice filled with cheer. He looked over at Bob's eldest son, who was carefully copying numbers into a ledger. "And good morning to you as well, young Peter. How are you both today?"

"We're well, sir. Thank you," Bob said, glancing at his son with a proud smile.

Scrooge nodded, stepping further into the room. "I'm glad to hear it. I thought I'd come by to see how things are going. And, Bob, I want you to know that the changes we spoke of are just the beginning. There is much more I intend to do for you and your family."

Bob's eyes glistened with gratitude, and he nodded. "Thank you, Mr. Scrooge. You've already done so much."

Scrooge waved a hand dismissively. "Nonsense, Bob. It's the least I can do. Now, let's get to work, shall we? There's a new year ahead, and I want it to be the best one yet for all of us."

Bob and Peter exchanged a glance, smiles spreading across their faces. Scrooge moved to his own desk, rolling up his sleeves as he prepared to dive into the day's work. The office, once a place of cold efficiency, now felt warm and full of promise. The future was bright, and Scrooge intended to embrace it fully, one kind act at a time.

Chapter 5

In the days that followed, Ebenezer Scrooge found himself caught up in a whirlwind of change—each moment an opportunity to make things right, to extend the warmth he had received from others. His old habits of isolation and self-interest were fading into a distant memory, replaced with the desire to truly engage with the people around him. The city that had once seemed gray and indifferent now felt vibrant, alive, filled with people who were slowly beginning to accept the new man he was becoming.

This particular morning, Scrooge awoke before dawn, the chill of winter creeping through his home as he dressed in the dim light. He wrapped his coat tightly around himself and, with a determined smile, set out into the streets of London. His mind was made up—today he would seek out some of his former clients, people he had treated poorly, and do what he could to amend his past mistakes.

The first destination on his list was Mr. Hargrove's textile shop. Scrooge had once been ruthless in his dealings with Mr. Hargrove, raising interest rates until the poor man was nearly forced to give up his business. Now, with his heart full of newfound resolve, Scrooge approached the modest shop, the bell above the door chiming softly as he entered.

Mr. Hargrove looked up from behind the counter, his eyes narrowing at the sight of Scrooge. His face tightened in fear, a mixture of suspicion and weariness etched in his features.

"Mr. Scrooge," Hargrove greeted him cautiously, setting down a bolt of fabric. "What brings you here today?"

Scrooge smiled warmly, removing his hat as he stepped forward. "Good morning, Mr. Hargrove. I hope you don't mind my dropping by unannounced. I've come to discuss our business arrangement."

Mr. Hargrove's brow furrowed, his skepticism evident. "Our arrangement?" he repeated, uncertainty in his voice.

Scrooge nodded, his gaze earnest and unwavering. "Indeed. You see, I've been reflecting on my past conduct—how I treated you, and others like you—and I realize I was far too harsh. I fear I caused you unnecessary hardship, and I wish to make amends."

Mr. Hargrove stared at him, clearly taken aback. He opened his mouth as if to respond, but seemed at a loss for words. Scrooge continued, his voice gentle.

"I have here new terms for your loan," Scrooge said, reaching into his coat to retrieve a folded piece of parchment. "Much more favorable terms, I assure you. I want to see you succeed, Mr. Hargrove—not live in fear of losing your livelihood."

He handed the parchment to Mr. Hargrove, whose hands trembled slightly as he took it. The shopkeeper's eyes widened as he read the new terms, and when he looked back at Scrooge, his expression had softened into one of disbelief and cautious hope.

"Mr. Scrooge… I don't know what to say," Hargrove murmured, his voice thick with emotion. "This is far more generous than I ever imagined."

Scrooge smiled and chuckled, feeling a warmth spread through his chest. "Say nothing, Mr. Hargrove. Just know that I am truly sorry for the way I treated you, and that I wish for your business to thrive."

Mr. Hargrove nodded, his eyes glistening. "Thank you, sir. This means the world to me and my family."

Scrooge placed a gentle hand on Mr. Hargrove's shoulder. "Then consider it a Christmas gift, and may your future be bright."

With a final nod, Scrooge left the shop, the bell chiming softly behind him. He stepped out into the cold morning, his heart feeling lighter than it had in years. There were many more people to whom he owed apologies and reparations, and he was determined to face each and every one of them.

His next destination was Mrs. Dempsey's bakery, a quaint little shop known for its freshly baked bread and sweet pastries. Scrooge remembered how, in the past, he had been relentless when Mrs. Dempsey had fallen behind on her payments, threatening foreclosure without a hint of compassion. Now, he intended to make things right.

As he approached the bakery, Scrooge could see Mrs. Dempsey through the window, arranging loaves of bread on the shelves. He pushed the door open, the small bell above it jingling to announce his arrival. Mrs. Dempsey looked up, her eyes widening at the sight of him. She straightened, her face guarded.

"Mr. Scrooge," she said, her voice wary. "What can I do for you?"

Scrooge smiled, removing his hat and stepping closer. "Good morning, Mrs. Dempsey. I realize my visit may come as a surprise, perhaps more of a shock, but I've come here today to apologize."

Mrs. Dempsey's expression shifted, confusion mingling with the wariness in her eyes. "Apologize?"

"Yes," Scrooge said, his voice sincere. "I was far too harsh with you in the past, and I deeply regret the stress I caused. You have a fine business here, and it deserves to flourish without the burden of unfair terms."

He reached into his coat once more, producing a piece of parchment similar to the one he had given Mr. Hargrove. "I've drawn up new terms for your loan, Mrs. Dempsey. Fair terms that will allow you to continue doing what you love without fear."

Mrs. Dempsey hesitated, then took the parchment from Scrooge, her eyes scanning the words. Slowly, her guarded expression began to soften, and tears welled in her eyes. "Mr. Scrooge… I don't know what to say. This is so… kind of you."

Scrooge's smile widened, and he gave a small nod. "Consider it my way of making amends. I only hope that you can forgive my past behavior."

Mrs. Dempsey wiped at her eyes with the corner of her apron, her voice trembling as she spoke. "Thank you, Mr. Scrooge. You've no idea how much this means to me."

Scrooge bowed his head slightly. "It is I who should be thanking you, Mrs. Dempsey, for giving me the chance to make things right."

With that, Scrooge turned and made his way out of the bakery, the bell chiming softly as the door closed behind him. He stood for a moment on the cobbled street, breathing in the crisp winter air. His heart felt lighter still, as though each act of kindness lifted a burden he had carried for far too long.

As the day continued, Scrooge visited several more businesses and individuals he had wronged. Each apology, each gesture of goodwill, seemed to chip away at the walls he had built around himself for so many years. The skeptical looks began to soften, the guarded expressions giving way to tentative smiles. It was not instantaneous, and he knew it would take time, but Scrooge was patient. He was committed to this path.

By the time the sun began to set, Scrooge found himself near the river, the water reflecting the orange and pink hues of the evening sky. He paused, leaning against the railing of a small bridge, watching as the day gave way to night. For the first time in his life, Ebenezer Scrooge felt truly at peace.

"Marley," he whispered, his breath misting in the cold air. "I hope you see this. I hope you know that I'm doing my best."

The wind rustled softly, as if in response, and Scrooge closed his eyes, a smile playing on his lips. He had been given a second chance, and he would not waste it. There was still much work to be done, and he was ready for whatever tomorrow would bring.

Later that afternoon, as the sun began to dip toward the horizon, Scrooge found himself walking past the old broker's house. The building loomed before him, its windows dark and cold, the paint peeling from years of neglect. A shiver ran down his spine as he remembered the ghostly vision he had witnessed—the men who spoke so callously of a recently deceased man, unaware that it was Scrooge himself they spoke of. He paused, staring up at the building, the memories flooding his mind.

He remembered the indifference in their voices, the way they had dismissed the dead man's life as meaningless, devoid of warmth or love. It had been a cruel but necessary wake-up call, a vision that had shaken him to his core and led him to the path he now walked.

Scrooge took a deep breath, his hands trembling slightly as he approached the entrance. He pushed open the door, the rusty hinges groaning in protest. Inside, the broker's house was as grim as he remembered—dim and cluttered, the air thick with the smell of dust and decay.

A few men sat around a table near the back, their voices low as they discussed matters of business. They looked up as Scrooge entered, their eyes widening in surprise. One of them—a man named Jenkins, whom Scrooge recognized from his earlier vision—stared at him, his brow furrowed.

"Mr. Scrooge?" Jenkins said, his voice tinged with confusion. "What brings you here?"

Scrooge stepped closer, his gaze steady. "Good afternoon, gentlemen," he greeted them, his tone calm. "I realize my visit may be unexpected, but I felt it was time to set a few things right."

The men exchanged puzzled glances, and Jenkins cleared his throat. "Set things right, sir?"

Scrooge nodded, his expression softening. "I know the kind of man I once was. I know what was said of me here—how little regard anyone had for my life, and rightly so. But I have changed.

And I wish to help, in whatever way I can, those who once suffered under my hand."

The room fell silent, the men staring at Scrooge as if they couldn't quite believe what they were hearing. Slowly, Jenkins rose to his feet, his eyes searching Scrooge's face.

"Are you saying… you wish to make amends, Mr. Scrooge?" Jenkins asked, his voice cautious.

"Yes," Scrooge replied, his voice firm. "I know it will take time for others to believe in my transformation, but I am committed. I will do whatever it takes to right my past wrongs."

Jenkins studied him for a long moment, then nodded slowly. "Very well, Mr. Scrooge. We'll see if your actions match your words."

Scrooge smiled, a sense of determination settling over him. "Thank you, Mr. Jenkins. I intend to prove it, not just to you, but to myself as well."

He turned and left the broker's house, stepping back out into the cold evening air. The sky was painted with the fading colors of dusk, and Scrooge felt a renewed sense of purpose. He knew there would be challenges ahead—that not everyone would be willing to forgive or forget—but he was ready to face them.

With every step he took, Ebenezer Scrooge moved further away from the man he had once been, and closer to the man he hoped to become.

Chapter 6

The morning sun peeked over the rooftops of London, casting a golden hue on the cobblestone streets below. Ebenezer Scrooge walked with purpose, his eyes bright, his spirits high. Today, he was ready to confront yet another part of his past—the very people who had once taken joy in the prospect of his demise. He had not forgotten the haunting visit with the Ghost of Christmas Yet to Come, where he had seen himself, dead and unlamented, discussed so casually at the broker's house.

He knew that these men of business had seen him as little more than a miser—a man whose life held no meaning beyond wealth. Today, he would show them that he was no longer that man. Although he visited the broker's house yesterday, he knew that many of the men he had deal with in the past had long left for the day. To further his transformation, another visit was necessary.

The broker's house loomed ahead, a relic of its former self. Ebenezer took time to notice its wooden beams sagged, the windows dirty and clouded with grime. Scrooge pushed the door open, the creak echoing through the dim interior. The air inside was thick with the smell of musty old ledgers and stale tobacco smoke. A group of men sat at a table near the back of the room, hunched over their cards, their faces shrouded in the dim light filtering through the filthy windows.

Scrooge approached, his footsteps soft but deliberate, until he stood before them. One of the men—Jenkins, who had been the most outspoken during that terrible vision—looked up, his eyes narrowing in suspicion as he recognized Scrooge.

"Mr. Scrooge," Jenkins said slowly, setting his cards down. The others looked up, their expressions hardening as they took in the sight of the man they had once spoken of so derisively.

"Gentlemen," Scrooge said, removing his hat and holding it respectfully before him. His voice was calm, without a hint of his former arrogance. "I imagine my presence here is a surprise."

Jenkins leaned back in his chair, crossing his arms over his chest. "You could say that," he replied, his tone skeptical. "What brings you to our humble establishment, Scrooge?"

Scrooge met Jenkins' gaze, his own steady and sincere. "I've come here because I remember the things that were said in this very room. I remember how my name was spoken, as if I was already gone—and I can't blame you for the way you spoke of me. The man I was then deserved nothing less."

Jenkins raised an eyebrow, glancing at the others. "You remember, do you?"

Scrooge nodded, a sad smile tugging at his lips. "I do. And I can't change the past. But I can change the man I am today. I've come here not to ask for your favor, but to offer my apologies. I was a man consumed by greed, with no thought for the lives of others. I lived in darkness, and I was blind to the pain I caused."

The room was silent, the other men exchanging glances, their expressions softening slightly as Scrooge spoke. He continued, his voice strong.

"I know I have much to atone for, and I do not expect instant forgiveness. I only hope that, in time, I may earn your respect—not as the miser I once was, but as a man who has learned the true value of life and kindness."

For a long moment, no one spoke. Jenkins studied Scrooge, his brow furrowed. Finally, he leaned forward, resting his elbows on the table. "You're serious about this, aren't you?"

"Yes," Scrooge replied simply. "I am."

Jenkins let out a long breath, shaking his head. "Well, I'll be. I never thought I'd live to see the day Ebenezer Scrooge would walk in here with an apology."

Scrooge smiled, a warmth filling his chest. "Perhaps it's a Christmas miracle, Mr. Jenkins. I've learned that it's never too late to change, as long as one is willing."

The other men nodded slowly, the tension in the room beginning to ease. Jenkins extended his hand across the table, his expression softening. "Well then, Mr. Scrooge, I suppose we'll just have to see how this new you turns out."

Scrooge took Jenkins' hand, shaking it firmly. "You have my word, Mr. Jenkins. I am a changed man, and I intend to prove it—one act of kindness at a time."

Jenkins nodded, a smile finally breaking across his face. "We'll hold you to that, Scrooge."

Scrooge placed his hat back on his head and gave the group a nod before turning and leaving the broker's house. As he stepped out into the fresh air, he felt a sense of peace settle over him.

He had faced his past, and though it was not easy, he knew it was necessary. He had taken another step toward becoming the man he wanted to be, and that brought him hope.

The afternoon sun had begun its slow descent, painting the sky in hues of orange and pink. Scrooge made his way through the streets, smiling at those he passed, tipping his hat to familiar faces. He had one more stop to make today—one that was long overdue.

He soon found himself in front of a modest brick building—a small charitable institution run by two gentlemen he had once turned away with scorn. He remembered their faces well, how they had approached him years ago, asking for donations for the poor, only to be dismissed cruelly. Now, he intended to make amends.

Scrooge knocked on the door, and after a moment, it opened to reveal one of the gentlemen—Mr. Smythe. His eyes widened in surprise at the sight of Scrooge standing there, a hesitant smile forming on his lips.

"Mr. Scrooge?" Smythe said, his voice filled with uncertainty. "What brings you here?"

"Good afternoon, Mr. Smythe," Scrooge greeted warmly. "I realize this may come as a shock, but I've come to apologize for my past behavior—and, if you'll allow it, to contribute to your cause."

Mr. Smythe blinked, clearly taken aback. "Contribute?"

Scrooge nodded, reaching into his coat and pulling out a small leather pouch. He handed it to Smythe, who opened it carefully, his eyes widening as he saw the coins inside.

"I know it cannot erase the past," Scrooge said softly, "but I hope it may help those in need. I am truly sorry for the way I treated you, and I wish to do better."

Mr. Smythe looked up at Scrooge, his eyes glistening. "This is… very generous, Mr. Scrooge. Thank you. It will make a great difference."

Scrooge smiled, a sense of fulfillment washing over him. "That is all I wish for. Thank you for giving me the opportunity to make things right."

Mr. Smythe nodded, a smile spreading across his face. "It's never too late to change, Mr. Scrooge. I believe you are proof of that."

Scrooge tipped his hat, his heart swelling with gratitude. "Thank you, Mr. Smythe. And a very Merry Christmas to you."

"Merry Christmas, Mr. Scrooge," Smythe replied, his voice warm.

As Scrooge walked away from the charitable institution, he felt lighter than he had in years. The burden of his past mistakes no longer felt as heavy, replaced by the joy of giving, of connecting with those around him. He had spent so much of his life alone, locked away from the world by his own greed and fear. Now, he was free—free to live, to love, to make a difference.

And as the sun set over London, Ebenezer Scrooge knew that this was only the beginning. The journey ahead was long, but he was ready to face it, one day at a time, with an open heart and a newfound sense of purpose.

Chapter 7

Ebenezer Scrooge had faced many of his past regrets, but there was one that had weighed on his heart more heavily than all the others: the loss of his beloved sister, Fan. He had long avoided the cemetery where she was laid to rest, unable to confront the sorrow and guilt that accompanied the memory of her untimely death. But now, as part of his journey of redemption, Scrooge knew it was time to visit her grave—to speak to her, to ask for her forgiveness.

The sun had just begun to rise as Scrooge made his way to the small cemetery on the outskirts of town. A thin layer of frost coated the ground, crunching softly beneath his boots as he walked between the rows of headstones. His breath was visible in the cold air, and his heart felt heavy with anticipation as he approached the simple marker that bore his sister's name.

He knelt down, brushing away some fallen leaves that had gathered around the base of the headstone. The letters carved into the stone were weathered, but still clearly read: *Fan Scrooge—Beloved Sister*. For a long moment, Scrooge simply stared at the stone, the memories of their childhood flooding back to him.

"Dear Fan," he whispered, his voice trembling. "It's been too long."

Tears welled in his eyes as he spoke, the weight of his emotions finally breaking through. "I've missed you so much, dear sister. I've carried so much regret, so much guilt for not being there for you as I should have. You were the light in my life, and I let that light fade away."

His shoulders shook as he began to cry, his tears falling onto the cold earth. He covered his face with his hands, the years of loneliness and pain pouring out in that quiet cemetery. He thought of all the times he had pushed her memory away, refusing to confront the pain of losing her. He had been so consumed by his own bitterness that he had forgotten the joy she had brought into his life.

"I'm so sorry, Fan," he sobbed. "I wish I could have done things differently. I wish I could have been the brother you deserved. But I promise you, I'm trying now. I'm trying to be better—to be the man you always believed I could be."

Scrooge stayed there for a long time, the tears flowing freely as he poured out his heart to his sister. Slowly, the weight began to lift, replaced by a sense of peace. He knew that he could never change the past, but he could honor her memory by living a life she would be proud of. He reached out, gently placing his hand on the headstone.

"I love you, Fan," he whispered. "And I will never forget you."

After a long moment, Scrooge rose to his feet, wiping his eyes with the back of his hand. He looked down at the grave one last time, a bittersweet smile tugging at his lips. "Until we meet again, dear sister."

He turned and walked away, his heart feeling lighter for having finally faced his sorrow. As he left the cemetery, Scrooge knew there was still one more part of his past he needed to confront—his lost love. The woman he had once dreamed of marrying, whose heart he had broken in his pursuit of wealth and power. He had often wondered what had become of her, whether she had found happiness after he had pushed her away.

Her name was Belle, and she had been the love of his life. Scrooge knew that seeking her out was a risk—that seeing her again might reopen old wounds. But he needed to know. He needed to see for himself that she had found the happiness he had been unable to give her.

Scrooge made his way through the streets of London, his heart pounding with a mixture of anticipation and dread. He had learned, through old acquaintances, that Belle had married and moved to a quiet part of the city. She had children now, a family of her own, and Scrooge hoped that she had found the joy she deserved.

The house was modest but well-kept, with a small garden out front. Scrooge stood at the gate, his eyes taking in the sight of the home that Belle had built for herself. Through the window, he could see her—Belle, older now but still as beautiful as he remembered. She was laughing, her face glowing with warmth, as she spoke to a group of children gathered around her. Scrooge's heart clenched at the sight, a bittersweet ache filling his chest.

He watched from a distance, a smile forming on his lips as he saw the happiness in her eyes. She had moved on, found a life full of love and laughter. And though a part of him still ached for what might have been, Scrooge knew that this was as it should be. Belle had found the happiness that he had been too blind to give her, and for that, he was grateful.

Scrooge stood there for a long moment, watching the scene unfold before him. He felt a sense of closure, a sense of peace in knowing that she was well. He had no right to intrude on her life now, no right to ask for anything more. She had moved on, and so must he.

With a deep breath, Scrooge turned away from the gate, his heart heavy but resolved. He walked back down the street, the sounds of children's laughter fading behind him. There was no room for regret now—only the promise of a better future, a future where he could make amends for the mistakes he had made.

As Scrooge made his way home, he felt a sense of calm settle over him. He had faced the ghosts of his past, both literal and metaphorical, and he had emerged from the darkness with a new sense of purpose. He could not change what had been, but he could shape what was to come. And he would do so with all the love and kindness that he had once withheld.

The evening sky was painted in deep shades of purple and blue as Scrooge approached his door. He paused, looking up at the stars that twinkled above, a smile playing on his lips.

"Thank you, Fan. Thank you, Belle," he whispered. "For everything." And with that, Ebenezer Scrooge stepped inside, ready to continue his journey of redemption, one day at a time.

CHAPTER 8

The morning dawned cold and crisp, a light frost blanketing the cobblestones of London. Ebenezer Scrooge awoke with a sense of purpose, though for once, it wasn't driven by any particular plan or appointment. Today, he felt an inexplicable urge to revisit a place he had not seen in decades—his old school, the place of so many bittersweet memories. The thought struck him as he dressed, a wistful smile tugging at his lips. He had spent too many Christmases there, alone and forgotten, until his sister Fan had changed everything. He wanted to see it again, to walk those old halls and reflect on the boy he had once been.

Bundled against the morning chill, Scrooge stepped out of his home, signaling for a passing carriage. The driver tipped his hat as Scrooge climbed in, settling into the worn leather seat. He gave the driver the directions to his old school, and the carriage rolled forward, the rhythmic clatter of hooves echoing through the narrow streets.

As the carriage made its way out of the bustling city and into the countryside, Scrooge found himself lost in thought. The landscape slowly changed, the cityscape giving way to rolling fields and sparse groves of trees. Memories flooded his mind—images of a lonely boy sitting at a desk, staring out at the snow-covered grounds while other children went home to be with their families. He could almost feel the chill of those old classrooms, the emptiness that had settled in his heart each year when no one came for him.

But then, there was the memory of Fan. Sweet, joyful Fan, bursting through the door with the news that their father had finally allowed him to come home for Christmas. Her smile had been like the sun breaking through the clouds, and Scrooge had never forgotten the warmth of her embrace as she led him away from that lonely place.

The carriage pulled to a stop, jolting Scrooge from his reverie. He looked out the window, his breath catching in his throat. The old schoolhouse stood before him, its stone walls weathered by time but still standing strong. Scrooge stepped out of the carriage, his boots crunching on the frost-covered ground as he approached the entrance. The building seemed smaller now, less imposing than it had in his childhood, but the memories it held were as vivid as ever.

He pushed open the heavy wooden door, the hinges groaning in protest. The corridor beyond was dimly lit, the air cool and still. Scrooge walked slowly, his footsteps echoing off the stone walls. He peered into the old classrooms, the rows of empty desks covered in a fine layer of dust. It was as if time had stood still here, the past lingering in every corner.

Scrooge paused at one particular classroom, his eyes drawn to a desk near the back—the very one where he had spent so many lonely hours. He stepped inside, running his fingers along the edge of the desk, his heart heavy with the memory of all the Christmases he had spent here, alone and forgotten. He closed his eyes, the ache of those days washing over him. But there was no bitterness now—only a deep sense of understanding. He had been a lonely child, but he was no longer a lonely man. He had the power to change things, to ensure that no child ever felt the way he had.

Suddenly, Scrooge heard a soft noise—a faint sniffle that broke the silence of the empty schoolhouse. He turned, his eyes scanning the room until they landed on a small figure huddled in the corner. A boy, no older than ten, sat with his knees drawn up to his chest, his face partially hidden by his arms. His clothes were worn and patched, his cheeks streaked with tears.

Scrooge's heart twisted at the sight. He approached slowly, kneeling down beside the boy. "Hello there, lad," he said gently, his voice barely above a whisper. "What's your name?"

The boy looked up, his eyes wide and fearful. He sniffled, wiping his nose with the back of his hand. "T-Timothy, sir," he replied, his voice trembling.

Scrooge smiled kindly, his eyes softening. "Timothy, eh? And what are you doing here all alone?"

The boy hesitated, glancing away. "I... I've no place to go, sir. They all went home for Christmas, but... no one came for me."

Scrooge felt a pang deep in his chest, the boy's words striking a chord that resonated with his own past. He reached out, placing a comforting hand on Timothy's shoulder. "Well, Timothy, it just so happens that I know a place where you'll be most welcome. Would you like to come with me?"

Timothy looked up, his eyes filled with a mixture of hope and uncertainty. "Truly, sir? You'd take me with you?"

Scrooge nodded, his smile widening. "Indeed, I would. No child should be alone at Christmas—or any time, for that matter. Come along, lad. Let's get you someplace warm."

Scrooge stood, holding out his hand to the boy. Timothy hesitated for a moment, then slipped his small hand into Scrooge's, allowing himself to be led out of the cold, empty schoolhouse. They made their way back to the carriage, Scrooge helping Timothy climb inside before following after him. He gave the driver new directions—this time to Fred's house. He knew his nephew would understand. Fred had a heart as big as London itself, and he would never turn away a child in need.

The ride back to the city was quiet, Timothy's head resting against Scrooge's side as he dozed off, exhausted from his ordeal. Scrooge looked down at the boy, a warmth spreading through his chest. He had once been this child—lost, forgotten, with no one to care for him. But now, he had the chance to change that, to make sure that Timothy knew he was not alone.

When they arrived at Fred's house, Scrooge gently shook Timothy awake. The boy blinked up at him, his eyes wide with curiosity as he looked at the grand house before them. Scrooge helped him out of the carriage, leading him up the steps to the front door. He knocked, and after a moment, the door swung open to reveal Fred, his face lighting up with surprise and joy at the sight of his uncle.

"Uncle Scrooge! What a pleasant surprise!" Fred exclaimed, his eyes then drifting to Timothy, a look of curiosity crossing his face. "And who is this young gentleman?"

Scrooge smiled, placing a gentle hand on Timothy's shoulder. "This is Timothy, Fred. I found him at my old school, alone. He has no place to go, and I was hoping you might take him in—at least until I can arrange something more permanent."

Fred's eyes softened, and he knelt down to Timothy's level, his smile warm and reassuring. "Well, Timothy, it's a pleasure to meet you. You're more than welcome to stay here with us. We'll make sure you're well taken care of."

Timothy looked up at Scrooge, his eyes shining with tears. "Thank you, sir," he whispered, his voice thick with emotion.

Scrooge knelt beside him, his own eyes misting. "You're very welcome, lad. You deserve all the joy and warmth this world has to offer."

Fred stood, extending his hand to Timothy. "Come along, Timothy. Let's get you settled in, shall we?"

Timothy took Fred's hand, allowing himself to be led inside. Scrooge watched them go, his heart swelling with a sense of fulfillment. He had once been the boy left behind, but now, he had the chance to be the one who reached out—a chance to change a life, to bring hope where there had once been none.

Fred turned back to Scrooge, a smile on his face. "Will you join us for breakfast, Uncle?"

Scrooge hesitated for a moment, then nodded, a smile spreading across his face. "I believe I will, Fred. Thank you."

He stepped inside, the warmth of Fred's home wrapping around him like a comforting embrace. As the door closed behind him, Scrooge felt a deep sense of peace settle over him. He was no longer the man he had once been—no longer the miser who had turned away from the world. He was a man reborn, determined to spread the light of kindness and compassion to all those he met.

And as he sat down to breakfast with his family—his true family—Ebenezer Scrooge knew that this was just the beginning. There were still many lives to touch, many wrongs to right, but he was ready. He had the love of his family, the memory of his sister, and the hope of a brighter future to guide him.

For the first time in his life, Scrooge truly understood the meaning of Christmas. It was not about wealth or power, but about love, compassion, and the simple act of reaching out to those in need. And he would carry that lesson with him, every day, for the rest of his life.

Chapter 9

Revisiting Marley's Legacy

The morning was cold and clear as Ebenezer Scrooge rose from his bed, a sense of determination settling in his heart. There was something that had been weighing on his mind—something that he had not yet faced since his transformation. It was time to confront the legacy of Jacob Marley, his old partner. Marley had been just as consumed by greed and ambition as Scrooge had once been, and together, they had forged a reputation built on ruthless business dealings. But Marley had also been the first to show him a way out of the darkness, even in death. Scrooge owed it to his old friend to make things right.

Scrooge dressed quickly, the chill of the winter morning seeping through his windowpanes. He wrapped himself in his warmest coat and set out into the bustling streets of London. His footsteps were brisk as he headed towards the old office he had once shared with Marley. The building loomed ahead, its facade as imposing as ever, but to Scrooge, it now seemed less intimidating, more a relic of the past than a place of power.

He stepped through the heavy door, the hinges groaning in protest. The office was quiet, the air thick with the scent of old paper and ink. Scrooge made his way to the back room, the place where he and Marley had conducted much of their business, making decisions that had left many people struggling under the weight of debt and despair. He paused at the desk, running his fingers over the smooth wood, memories flooding back—memories of long hours spent tallying profits and calculating how to extract the most from their clients.

Scrooge opened a drawer, pulling out a stack of old documents. The yellowed pages were filled with names and numbers, each one a reminder of the people they had once treated so callously. He flipped through them slowly, his heart heavy with regret. These were more than just records—they were the stories of lives they had affected, families they had torn apart in the name of profit.

One name caught his eye—Mr. Howell. Scrooge remembered the man well, remembered the way he had begged for leniency when his business had struggled during a harsh winter. But Scrooge and Marley had shown no mercy, raising interest rates until Mr. Howell had been forced to sell everything he owned. Scrooge felt a pang of guilt, the memory of Mr. Howell's desperation flashing before his eyes.

Scrooge knew what he had to do. He gathered the documents, tucking them under his arm as he left the office. He stepped out into the crisp morning air, his breath visible in the cold. He had to find Mr. Howell, to make amends for the wrongs he had done.

It took some time, but eventually, Scrooge found Mr. Howell's address. The man now lived in a modest home on the outskirts of the city, a far cry from the prosperous business he had once owned. Scrooge approached the door, his heart pounding with anticipation. He knocked, the sound echoing through the quiet street.

The door creaked open, and there stood Mr. Howell, his face lined with age and weariness. His eyes widened in surprise at the sight of Scrooge, a mix of confusion and apprehension crossing his features.

"Mr. Scrooge?" Howell said, his voice hesitant. "What brings you here?"

Scrooge removed his hat, holding it before him. "Good morning, Mr. Howell. I realize this visit is unexpected, but I've come to speak with you about our past dealings."

Howell's brow furrowed, his gaze wary. "Our past dealings?"

"Yes," Scrooge nodded, his voice softening. "I've been doing a great deal of reflection lately, and I've come to realize just how much harm I caused you, Mr. Howell. I was blinded by greed, and I showed no compassion when you needed it most. For that, I am truly sorry."

Mr. Howell blinked, clearly taken aback. He opened his mouth to respond but seemed at a loss for words. Scrooge continued, his voice filled with sincerity.

"I've brought with me the documents from our dealings," Scrooge said, holding out the stack of papers. "I wish to forgive any remaining debt you owe, and I would like to help you rebuild what you lost. It's the least I can do after all the pain I caused."

Mr. Howell stared at the documents, then looked up at Scrooge, his eyes misting with emotion. "Mr. Scrooge... I don't know what to say. This is... beyond anything I could have hoped for."

Scrooge smiled, a warmth spreading through his chest. "You need say nothing at all, Mr. Howell. I only hope that you can find it in your heart to forgive me."

Howell nodded slowly, his expression softening. "I... I think I can, Mr. Scrooge. Thank you. This means more to me than you could ever know."

Scrooge reached out, placing a gentle hand on Howell's shoulder. "Then consider this a new beginning, for both of us."

With that, Scrooge handed the documents to Howell, who accepted them with trembling hands. Scrooge nodded, tipping his hat before turning to leave. As he walked away, he felt a sense of peace settle over him. He had taken yet another step in his journey of redemption, and it filled him with hope for the future.

The day was still young, and Scrooge knew there was more he could do. He made his way back to the heart of the city, his mind turning to the people he had once dismissed so easily—the workers, the families, the individuals who had struggled under the weight of his and Marley's demands. It was time to help them, to show them that he had changed, not just in words but in actions.

Scrooge found himself standing before a modest building—a soup kitchen, where the less fortunate came for a warm meal and a kind word. He stepped inside, the warmth of the room enveloping him as he looked around. The people inside were a mix of young and old, their faces lined with the struggles of life. Scrooge felt a pang of regret, knowing that he had once turned a blind eye to their suffering.

He approached the woman who ran the kitchen, a kind-looking lady with a warm smile. She looked up as he approached, her eyes widening slightly in surprise.

"Mr. Scrooge?" she said, her voice tinged with curiosity. "What brings you here?"

Scrooge smiled, removing his hat. "Good morning. I've come to offer my assistance, if you'll have it. I wish to help, in any way I can."

The woman blinked, clearly taken aback. "Help? Why… of course, Mr. Scrooge. We could always use an extra pair of hands."

Scrooge nodded, rolling up his sleeves. "Then consider me at your service."

He spent the next several hours serving food, speaking with the people who came through the doors, and listening to their stories. He laughed with them, offered words of comfort, and shared in their struggles. It was a humbling experience, one that filled him with a sense of purpose he had never known before.

As the day came to a close, Scrooge stepped outside, the chill of the evening air biting at his skin. He looked up at the darkening sky, a smile spreading across his face. He had spent so much of his life taking from others, but now, he was finally giving back. And it felt wonderful.

He thought of Marley, of the chains that had bound him in death—chains forged by their own greed and selfishness. Scrooge knew that he could never change Marley's fate, but he could honor his memory by living a better life. A life filled with compassion, kindness, and love for those around him.

As he walked, Scrooge chuckled softly to himself. "Those spirits really did their job well," he mused, shaking his head with a smile. "They made sure I wouldn't forget the lessons they taught me."

Chapter 10

Community Outreach

The following day, Ebenezer Scrooge awoke with a renewed sense of determination. He had begun to make amends for the wrongs of his past, but he knew that his journey was far from over. There were still many people in the community who needed help, and Scrooge was eager to do whatever he could to assist them. He had spent too many years ignoring the needs of those around him, and now he wanted to dedicate himself to being an active part of the community.

After a quick breakfast, Scrooge dressed warmly and set out into the bustling streets of London. The morning air was crisp, and the city was alive with the sounds of carriages, street vendors, and people going about their day. Scrooge walked with purpose, his eyes scanning the faces of those he passed, taking in the life and activity of the city that he had once seen only as a means to profit.

His first stop was a modest workshop owned by a young couple, Mr. and Mrs. Thompson. The Thompsons had taken out a loan from Scrooge years ago, and though they had been diligent in their payments, they had struggled to make ends meet. Scrooge knew he had been unyielding with them, raising the interest on their loan and making their lives unnecessarily difficult. Today, he hoped to make things right.

Scrooge knocked on the door of the workshop, and after a moment, Mrs. Thompson opened it, her eyes widening in surprise at the sight of him. She was a petite woman with kind eyes, though they were lined with weariness.

"Mr. Scrooge?" she said, her voice tinged with confusion. "What brings you here? I made my payment on time."

Scrooge smiled warmly, removing his hat. "Good morning, Mrs. Thompson. I realize my visit is unexpected, but I've come to speak with you and your husband about the loan you took out some years ago."

Mrs. Thompson's brow furrowed, and she called over her shoulder, "James, it's Mr. Scrooge."

A moment later, Mr. Thompson appeared, wiping his hands on a rag. He was a tall man, his face lined with stress, though his eyes held a glimmer of hope. "Mr. Scrooge," he greeted, his voice cautious. "What can we do for you?"

Scrooge looked from one to the other, his smile softening. "It's not what you can do for me, but what I can do for you," he said. "I've come to forgive the remaining balance of your loan, and to apologize for the hardship I caused you both. I know I made things more difficult than they needed to be, and for that, I am truly sorry."

The Thompsons exchanged a stunned glance, their eyes widening. Mrs. Thompson's hand flew to her mouth, her eyes misting with tears. "You... you're forgiving our debt?" she whispered.

Scrooge nodded. "Yes, indeed. Consider it my way of making amends. I want you both to be able to grow your business and provide for your family without the burden of debt hanging over you."

Mr. Thompson's eyes filled with tears, and he reached out to shake Scrooge's hand. "Mr. Scrooge, I don't know how to thank you. This... this means everything to us."

Scrooge took his hand, shaking it firmly. "No thanks are necessary. Just know that I am committed to being a better man, and I hope that you can forgive my past mistakes."

Mrs. Thompson stepped forward, her eyes shining with gratitude. "Of course, Mr. Scrooge. You have no idea how much this means to us. Thank you."

Scrooge smiled, tipping his hat before turning to leave. "I wish you both all the best. May your business thrive and your family prosper."

As he walked away from the workshop, Scrooge felt a sense of fulfillment settle over him. He had taken another step toward righting the wrongs of his past, and it filled him with hope for the future. But there was still more work to be done.

Scrooge continued his journey through the city, stopping at various businesses and homes where he knew he had caused harm. He forgave debts, offered assistance, and apologized for his past behavior. Some people were skeptical, their eyes narrowing as they listened to his words, but Scrooge remained patient. He knew that trust could not be rebuilt overnight, and he was willing to do whatever it took to prove that he had truly changed.

Later that afternoon, Scrooge found himself standing before a small orphanage on the edge of the city. The building was old, its bricks weathered by time, but the sound of children's laughter could be heard from within. Scrooge hesitated for a moment, then took a deep breath and knocked on the door.

A woman in her fifties opened the door, her face lined with years of care but her eyes warm and kind. "May I help you, sir?" she asked, her voice gentle.

Scrooge removed his hat, smiling. "Good afternoon, madam. My name is Ebenezer Scrooge. I've come to see if there's anything I can do to help."

The woman's eyes widened in surprise, and she stepped back to allow him inside. "Mr. Scrooge? The children's benefactor?"

Scrooge blinked, a little taken aback. "Benefactor?"

"Yes," she nodded, a smile spreading across her face. "You see, a generous donation was made in your name just after Christmas—enough to keep us running for the entire year."

Scrooge's eyes softened, realizing that perhaps one of the spirits had done this on his behalf. He felt a warmth in his chest, a smile spreading across his face. "Well, that's wonderful to hear. But I'd still like to offer my assistance, however I can."

The woman led Scrooge through the orphanage, introducing him to the children. He spent the afternoon with them, playing games, sharing stories, and listening to their laughter. It was a joyous experience, one that filled him with a sense of purpose and fulfillment he had never known before.

As the sun began to set, Scrooge made his way back home, his heart full. He had seen firsthand the impact that kindness and generosity could have, and it only strengthened his resolve to continue down this path. He knew that there would always be those who doubted him, those who could not believe in his transformation, but he was prepared to prove them wrong—one day at a time.

As he walked, Scrooge couldn't help but chuckle to himself, shaking his head. "Those spirits," he murmured, a smile playing on his lips. "They truly did their job well."

With each step, Ebenezer Scrooge moved further away from the man he had once been, and closer to the man he hoped to become—a man filled with compassion, love, and a desire to make the world a better place for all.

Chapter 11

A Visit to Bob Cratchit's Home

The morning was bright, a golden sun illuminating the frost-covered streets of London, and Ebenezer Scrooge felt an excitement he had not known in years. Today, he was going to visit Bob Cratchit and his family. Scrooge had already given Bob a raise and promised to help support Tiny Tim's medical needs, but he wanted to do more. He wanted to get to know

Bob's family—to share in their joy and to bring a bit of cheer to their home.

Scrooge set out from his home, wrapped warmly against the chill, carrying a basket filled with gifts. The streets were bustling with people going about their day, and Scrooge greeted them all with a smile and a cheerful "Good morning!" The transformation in his demeanor was evident to those who recognized him—where once they had avoided his gaze, they now returned his greetings with warmth and curiosity.

When he arrived at the Cratchit residence, Scrooge paused for a moment, taking in the modest but well-kept home. The sound of children laughing drifted through the door, and Scrooge's heart swelled with emotion. He knocked gently, and after a moment, the door swung open to reveal Bob Cratchit, his eyes widening in surprise.

"Mr. Scrooge!" Bob exclaimed, a smile breaking across his face. "This is an unexpected pleasure. Please, come in!"

Scrooge beamed, stepping inside and handing Bob the basket of gifts. "Good morning, Bob. I hope I'm not intruding, but I wanted to bring a few things for the family—and to see how you're all getting along."

Bob's eyes glistened as he accepted the basket, his voice thick with emotion. "Thank you, sir. You're too kind. Please, come into the sitting room."

Scrooge followed Bob into the cozy sitting room, where a fire crackled merrily in the hearth. The room was filled with warmth and love, the kind of atmosphere that Scrooge had rarely experienced in his own home. Mrs. Cratchit stood by the fire, her face lighting up as she saw their guest.

"Mr. Scrooge!" she greeted, her voice filled with warmth. "What a wonderful surprise."

Scrooge smiled, bowing his head slightly. "Mrs. Cratchit, it is a pleasure to see you. I've brought some gifts for the children, if you don't mind."

Mrs. Cratchit's eyes filled with tears, and she nodded. "Thank you, Mr. Scrooge. You are far too generous."

Scrooge turned to the children, who were gathered around, their eyes wide with curiosity. He knelt down, opening the basket and pulling out a small toy for each of them—a wooden horse for Peter, a doll for Martha, and a set of colorful marbles for the younger children. Finally, he took out a beautifully carved wooden cane, handing it to Tiny Tim, who sat by the fire, his eyes shining with delight.

"This is for you, Tim," Scrooge said softly, his voice filled with affection. "I thought it might help you get around a bit more easily."

Tiny Tim's face lit up with joy, and he took the cane in his small hands, his voice trembling as he spoke. "Thank you, Mr. Scrooge. It's beautiful."

Scrooge felt a lump form in his throat, and he reached out to ruffle Tim's hair. "You are most welcome, my boy. I want you to know that I am here for you and your family—whatever you need."

Bob cleared his throat, his voice filled with emotion. "Mr. Scrooge, I cannot thank you enough for everything you've done for us. You've changed our lives."

Scrooge stood, his eyes misting over. "No, Bob. It is you and your family who have changed mine. You have shown me what true kindness and love look like, and for that, I am forever grateful."

The Cratchits invited Scrooge to stay for lunch, and he gladly accepted. He sat at their modest table, sharing a simple but hearty meal, and for the first time in many years, Scrooge felt truly at home. The laughter of the children, the warmth of the fire, and the love that filled the room wrapped around him like a comforting embrace.

As they ate, Scrooge listened to the children's stories, their laughter infectious, and he found himself joining in, his heart lighter than it had been in decades. He marveled at how much joy could be found in the simplest of moments, in the company of good people. He watched as Tiny Tim spoke animatedly with his siblings, his eyes bright with hope, and Scrooge felt a deep sense of fulfillment.

After lunch, Scrooge and Bob sat by the fire, watching the children play. Mrs. Cratchit had gone to the kitchen to prepare some tea, and Scrooge took the opportunity to speak with Bob about the future.

"Bob," Scrooge began, his voice gentle, "I want to ensure that your family is well taken care of, not just now, but in the years to come. I've been thinking about how I might help, and I would like to set up a fund for Tiny Tim's medical care—whatever he needs, for as long as he needs it."

Bob's eyes filled with tears, and he blinked rapidly, his voice thick with emotion. "Mr. Scrooge, I… I don't know what to say. You have already done so much for us."

Scrooge reached out, placing a hand on Bob's shoulder. "Nonsense, Bob. It is the least I can do. Tim is a remarkable boy, and he deserves every chance at a happy, healthy life. And I want you to know that you will always have my support."

Scrooge smiled warmly, then leaned closer to Bob. "In fact, Bob, I have already arranged for a surgeon to examine Tiny Tim," he said gently. "I want to ensure that he receives the best care available. The prognosis is that it will be a serious operation, with no guarantee of success, but I believe we must give Tim every chance we can."

Bob's eyes widened, and his voice trembled. "A surgeon, sir? You have done this for us?"

Scrooge nodded. "Yes, Bob. I know it's a difficult decision, but I want to give Tim the chance he deserves. It is, of course, up to you and Mrs. Cratchit whether you wish to proceed."

Bob swallowed hard, emotion thick in his voice. "We will do whatever it takes to help Tim, Mr. Scrooge. We... we are so grateful for everything you've done."

Scrooge smiled, his own eyes misting over. "It is I who should be thanking you, Bob. You and your family have given me a gift greater than any I could ever give—a second chance at life."

The afternoon passed in a blur of laughter and warmth, and as the sun began to dip below the horizon, Scrooge reluctantly rose to leave. He shook Bob's hand firmly, hugged Mrs. Cratchit, and ruffled the children's hair one last time before stepping out into the cold evening air.

As he walked home, Scrooge felt a deep sense of peace. He had spent so many years in darkness, cut off from the world and from the love of others, but now, he was finally part of something greater. He had a family—a true family—and it filled his heart with a joy he had never thought possible.

The streets of London were quiet as Scrooge made his way back to his home, the stars twinkling above. He looked up at the sky, a smile spreading across his face as he thought of the Cratchits, gathered around their fire, and of Tiny Tim, his eyes shining with hope.

"For the first time in my life," Scrooge whispered to himself, his voice filled with emotion, "I understand what Christmas truly means. It is not about wealth or power, but about love, compassion, and the joy of being together."

And as he stepped through the door of his home, Scrooge knew that he would carry that lesson with him, every day, for the rest of his life. The spirit of Christmas was not just for one day—it was something to be cherished, nurtured, and shared, every single day of the year.

With that thought warming his heart, Ebenezer Scrooge settled into his armchair by the fire, a contented smile on his face. He knew that the journey ahead would not always be easy, but he was ready—ready to live a life filled with love, generosity, and hope for the future.

Chapter 12

The Spirit of Christmas Year-Round

The days following his visit to the Cratchit household brought a new sense of purpose to Ebenezer Scrooge. He had begun to understand that his transformation was not just a matter of words or promises, but of daily action, of making an impact in the lives of those around him. He was no longer content to simply watch the world from his window—he wanted to be a part of it, to spread the spirit of Christmas far beyond the confines of one holiday season.

One morning, Scrooge awoke with an idea that filled him with excitement. He had heard of a small school on the outskirts of the city that was struggling to keep its doors open. It served children whose families could not afford private education, offering them a chance at a better future. Scrooge had never taken much interest in education before, but now he saw it as an opportunity to make a real difference—an opportunity to give back to the community in a meaningful way.

After a quick breakfast, Scrooge dressed in his finest coat and set out for the school, a determined look in his eyes. He hired a carriage, the ride taking him away from the bustling heart of London and into the quieter, more rural areas. As the city gave way to open fields and modest cottages, Scrooge felt a sense of calm settle over him, the beauty of the countryside reminding him of simpler times.

When he arrived at the school, he was greeted by the headmaster, a kind but weary-looking man named Mr. Stevenson. The school building was old and in need of repair, the paint peeling from the walls and the roof showing signs of wear. Scrooge could see the children playing in the yard, their laughter echoing through the crisp morning air, and he knew that this place was worth saving.

"Mr. Scrooge," Mr. Stevenson said, his voice filled with surprise as he shook Scrooge's hand. "I must admit, I was quite astonished when I received word of your visit. To what do we owe the honor?"

Scrooge smiled warmly, his eyes scanning the yard where the children played. "Mr. Stevenson, I've come to offer my assistance. I understand that your school has been struggling, and I would like to help. I wish to provide the funds needed for repairs, as well as anything else you may require to continue your important work."

Mr. Stevenson's eyes widened, and for a moment, he seemed at a loss for words. "Mr. Scrooge, this… this is more than I could have ever hoped for. The children… they deserve so much, and I've done my best, but…" His voice trailed off, emotion thick in his throat.

Scrooge placed a reassuring hand on the headmaster's shoulder. "You've done a wonderful job, Mr. Stevenson. And now, I'd like to ensure that these children have every opportunity for a bright future. Please, let me know what you need, and I will make it happen."

Tears filled Mr. Stevenson's eyes, and he nodded, his voice barely above a whisper. "Thank you, Mr. Scrooge. You have no idea what this means to us."

Scrooge spent the morning touring the school, speaking with the teachers and meeting the children. He saw their bright, eager faces, their curiosity and excitement for learning, and he knew he was making the right decision. He made arrangements for repairs to begin immediately, and he promised to provide new books, supplies, and even warm clothing for the winter.

The children gathered around him as he spoke, their eyes wide with wonder as they listened to his plans. One little girl, her face framed by dark curls, looked up at him with a shy smile. "Mr. Scrooge," she said softly, "are you Father Christmas?"

Scrooge chuckled, kneeling down to meet her eye level. "No, my dear, I am not Santa Claus. But I suppose I've learned that we can all be a bit like him, if we choose to be kind and generous."

The girl smiled, her eyes shining with delight, and Scrooge felt his heart swell with emotion. He had spent so many years closed off from the world, but now he saw the beauty in connection, in giving without expecting anything in return.

After leaving the school, Scrooge made his way to his nephew Fred's home. Fred had always been a beacon of warmth and kindness, even when Scrooge had pushed him away. Now, Scrooge wanted to share his plans with his nephew—to invite Fred to be a part of his mission to bring hope and joy to those in need.

Fred greeted his uncle with open arms, his face lighting up with joy at the sight of him. "Uncle Scrooge! What a wonderful surprise. Please, come in."

Scrooge stepped inside, the warmth of Fred's home wrapping around him like a comforting embrace. They settled in the sitting room, Fred's wife Clara joining them, her smile just as welcoming as her husband's.

"Fred, Clara," Scrooge began, his voice filled with excitement, "I've just returned from a visit to a small school on the outskirts of the city. They were in need of help, and I've decided to provide the funds to keep them going. But I need your help as well. I want to do more—much more—for our community. There are so many people in need, and I believe that together, we can make a real difference."

Fred's eyes shone with admiration, and he reached out to take his uncle's hand. "Uncle Ebenezer, I am so proud of you. Of course, we will help in any way we can. What did you have in mind?"

Scrooge smiled, his heart swelling with gratitude. "I was thinking that we could organize a community event—something to bring everyone together, to celebrate the new year and to share in the spirit of giving. We could raise funds for those in need, provide food and warmth for the less fortunate. I want to show everyone that the spirit of Christmas is not just for one day, but for every day."

Clara nodded, her eyes misting with emotion. "That sounds wonderful, Uncle. We would be honored to help."

Scrooge's smile widened, a sense of fulfillment washing over him. "Thank you, both of you. Together, I believe we can do something truly special."

The rest of the afternoon was spent planning the event, their ideas flowing freely as they discussed how best to bring the community together. Scrooge felt a sense of belonging that he had never known before—he was not alone, but part of something greater, something filled with love and hope.

As the sun began to set, Scrooge made his way home, his heart light with anticipation for what lay ahead. He had spent so many years in darkness, but now he was surrounded by light—by the love of his family, the hope of the children he had met, and the promise of a brighter future.

When he arrived home, Scrooge sat by the fire, a contented smile on his face. He thought of the journey he had taken, the changes he had made, and the people he had touched along the way. He knew that his work was far from over, but he was ready—ready to face each new day with an open heart and a spirit of generosity.

"For the first time in my life," Scrooge whispered to himself, his voice filled with emotion, "I truly understand the meaning of Christmas. It is not about wealth or power, but about love, compassion, and the joy of giving. One little girl Jacob, even thought I might be Father Christmas."

And with that thought warming his heart, Ebenezer Scrooge looked forward to the future—a future filled with hope, love, and the spirit of Christmas, every single day of the year.

Chapter 13

Visiting the Poorhouse

Ebenezer Scrooge awoke with a somber determination. His mind had been restless the night before, recalling the visions shown to him by the Ghost of Christmas Yet to Come. Those images of hopelessness, fear, and a future devoid of compassion still lingered in his memory. He had made great strides in changing his own fate, but he knew there was more work to be done—more people whose lives he could help improve.

After a simple breakfast, Scrooge wrapped himself in his heavy winter coat and ventured out into the cold streets of London. He had heard whispers of the poorhouse, where those who could not pay their debts were crammed together, stripped of dignity and hope. He knew it was time to see the place for himself, to confront yet another consequence of his former ways.

The poorhouse stood in the shadow of a factory, its stone facade darkened by soot and grime. The building was imposing, with narrow windows that seemed to trap the souls within rather than let in the light. As Scrooge approached, the sounds of coughing and muted voices reached his ears, each sound a reminder of the people who were suffering inside.

Scrooge pushed open the heavy door, the creaking hinges echoing down the narrow hallway. The air inside was stale, thick with the scent of despair. Rows of beds lined the cramped room, each one occupied by someone who had been brought low by circumstance—men, women, and even children, their eyes hollow from exhaustion and hopelessness.

Scrooge's heart clenched at the sight. He had seen many people struggling over the years, but to witness them confined like this was something else entirely. He walked slowly through the room, his eyes taking in the gaunt faces, the ragged clothing, and the hopeless expressions. He knew that his own greed, and the system he had once supported, had contributed to this misery.

He approached the overseer, a stern-looking man with a harsh expression who stood by the door, watching the residents with a critical eye. Scrooge cleared his throat, drawing the overseer's attention.

"Good day," Scrooge said, his voice firm. "I am Ebenezer Scrooge, and I've come to see how I might help these people."

The overseer's eyes narrowed, a flicker of recognition crossing his features. "Mr. Scrooge? I must admit, I'm surprised to see you here. I wasn't aware you were one to concern yourself with such matters. If I recall, weren't you concerned in the past about the efficiency of our poor houses?"

Scrooge ignored the implied criticism, his gaze steady. "That was true once, but it is no longer the case. I want to know why these people are left in such conditions, and I intend to do something about it."

The overseer hesitated, then shrugged. "These folks are debtors, Mr. Scrooge. They're here because they have nowhere else to go. The law is clear on such matters."

Scrooge frowned, his eyes drifting over the crowded room. "And is the law also clear that they must be treated without dignity? That they must live without hope?"

The overseer said nothing, and Scrooge shook his head. He turned back to the residents, his heart aching. He could see the pain etched in their faces, and he knew that he could not walk away without doing something—anything—to help them.

"Please gather everyone together," Scrooge said, his voice carrying through the room. The overseer's brow furrowed in confusion, but he nodded, moving to gather the residents.

As the people gathered before him, Scrooge took a deep breath, his heart pounding. He looked out at the faces before him, each one marked by hardship, and he felt a deep sense of responsibility.

"My friends," Scrooge began, his voice gentle but firm, "I know that many of you are here because of debts—debts that have kept you bound to this place, without hope of a future. I am here today to tell you that those debts will be forgiven. I will personally ensure that each of you is released from this burden, so that you may begin again."

A murmur rippled through the crowd, disbelief mingling with hope. Scrooge continued, his eyes softening as he spoke. "But I do not wish to stop there. I know that freedom from debt is only the beginning. I want each of you to have the opportunity to rebuild your lives, to learn a trade, to find meaningful work. My nephew, Fred, and I are establishing a training school—one that will provide you with the skills you need to succeed. And once you have completed your training, we will help you find apprenticeships and employment."

Tears filled the eyes of many in the crowd, their faces brightening with hope that had long been absent. A young mother stepped forward, her voice trembling as she spoke. "Mr. Scrooge… do you mean it? We will truly be free?"

Scrooge nodded, his eyes misting over as he looked at her. "Yes, my dear. You will all be free. And you will have the chance to build a future for yourselves—a future filled with hope and opportunity."

Yes, my dear. You will all be free. And you will have the chance to build a future for yourselves—a future filled with hope and opportunity. "Thank you, Mr. Scrooge. You have given us a miracle."

Scrooge smiled, his heart swelling with emotion. He had once been a man who had cared only for his own wealth, his own comfort, but now he saw the true power of generosity. It was not enough to simply give money—true change required action, compassion, and a willingness to lift others up.

After ensuring that the arrangements were in place, Scrooge left the poorhouse, the cold winter air filling his lungs as he stepped outside. Fred was waiting for him by the carriage, his eyes filled with curiosity.

"How did it go, Uncle?" Fred asked, his voice gentle.

Scrooge smiled, a tear escaping down his cheek. "It went well, Fred. I've forgiven their debts, and I've told them about our training program. We're going to give them a chance—a real chance—to build better lives."

Fred's face lit up with admiration, and he placed a hand on his uncle's shoulder. "I'm proud of you, Uncle Ebenezer. You've come so far, and you're making such a difference."

Scrooge nodded, his heart filled with gratitude. "I couldn't have done it without you, Fred. Together, we will ensure that the spirit of Christmas lives on—not just today, but every day."

As they climbed into the carriage and made their way back to the city, Scrooge looked out at the passing streets, his heart light. He had seen the darkness that his greed had wrought, but now he was determined to bring light, hope, and opportunity to those who needed it most.

For the first time in his life, Ebenezer Scrooge truly understood the meaning of redemption. It was not just about changing oneself, but about lifting others up—about ensuring that no one was left behind, that everyone had the chance to live with dignity, hope, and love.

Chapter 14

The New Year Celebration

The days leading up to the New Year were busy and full of anticipation for Ebenezer Scrooge, Fred, and the rest of the community. The plans for the New Year celebration had taken on a life of their own, transforming into something much bigger than Scrooge had initially imagined. The excitement was palpable in the air, and Scrooge found himself working alongside friends and neighbors—people who had once shunned him, but now embraced him as one of their own.

Fred and Clara had taken charge of organizing much of the event, their enthusiasm infectious. Clara had arranged for musicians to play, while Fred coordinated the food and decorations. Scrooge, for his part, made sure that everyone who wanted to attend could do so, providing transportation for those who lived far away and ensuring that no one was left behind.

The day of the celebration dawned crisp and clear, the sky a brilliant blue as the sun shone down on the snow-covered streets. The town square had been transformed into a place of joy and festivity—garlands of evergreen adorned the lampposts, and colorful ribbons fluttered in the breeze. Tables were set up, laden with food and drink, and a large fir tree stood in the center of the square, its branches decorated with candles that would be lit as night fell.

Scrooge stood at the edge of the square, watching as people began to gather. His heart swelled with emotion as he took in the scene before him—the laughter, the smiles, the sense of community that filled the air. It was everything he had hoped for and more.

Fred approached, a broad smile on his face as he clapped his uncle on the shoulder. "It's quite the sight, isn't it, Uncle Ebenezer?" he said, his voice filled with pride.

Scrooge nodded, his eyes misting over. "It is indeed, Fred. I could never have imagined anything like this. To think that I once spent my days alone, without a thought for anyone else… and now, to be surrounded by so much love and joy." He paused, his voice thick with emotion. "It's a miracle, Fred. A true miracle."

Fred smiled, his eyes shining with admiration. "And it's all because of you, Uncle. You've brought us all together, and you've shown us what the true spirit of Christmas is all about."

As the afternoon turned into evening, the celebration reached its peak. The musicians played lively tunes, and people danced in the square, their laughter ringing out into the night. Children ran between the tables, their faces flushed with excitement, and Scrooge watched them with a smile, his heart full.

As the candles on the great fir tree were lit, casting a warm glow over the square, Fred stepped forward, raising his hand to call for attention. The crowd quieted, turning to face him, their faces filled with anticipation.

"Friends, neighbors," Fred began, his voice carrying across the square, "thank you all for being here tonight. This celebration is about more than just welcoming a new year—it is about hope, about community, and about the spirit of giving. My uncle, Ebenezer Scrooge, has something he would like to share with you all."

Fred stepped back, gesturing for Scrooge to take his place. Scrooge hesitated for a moment, then stepped forward, his heart pounding as he looked out at the crowd. He had never been one for public speaking, but tonight was different—tonight, he had something worth saying.

"My friends," Scrooge began, his voice trembling slightly, "I want to thank each and every one of you for being here tonight. This celebration is a testament to the power of love, of compassion, and of the spirit of Christmas. It is a testament to the fact that it is never too late to change, to become a better person, and to make a difference in the lives of others."

He paused, his eyes scanning the crowd, taking in the faces of those who had once viewed him with disdain but now looked at him with warmth and respect. "I have spent many years of my life in darkness, consumed by greed and selfishness. But thanks to the kindness of others—thanks to people like my dear nephew Fred, and all of you—I have found a new purpose. I have found joy in giving, in helping others, and in being part of this wonderful community."

Scrooge took a deep breath, his voice growing stronger. "And so, tonight, I want to announce that Fred and I will be establishing a community fund—one that will provide support to those in need, not just during the holidays, but throughout the entire year. We will also be expanding the training program we've started, ensuring that everyone has the opportunity to learn, to work, and to build a better future for themselves and their families."

A cheer rose from the crowd, their faces lighting up with joy and hope. Scrooge smiled, his heart swelling with emotion as he continued. "This is my promise to you all—that I will do everything in my power to make this community a place of love, of hope, and of opportunity. A place where no one is left behind, and where the spirit of Christmas lives on every single day."

The crowd erupted in applause, their cheers echoing through the square. Fred stepped forward, wrapping his arms around his uncle in a warm embrace. "Well said, Uncle Ebenezer," he whispered, his voice thick with emotion. "Well said."

As the evening wore on, Scrooge found himself surrounded by friends and neighbors, their words of gratitude and admiration filling his ears. He spoke with each of them, listening to their stories, their hopes for the future, and he felt a deep sense of fulfillment. He had once been a man who had cared only for his own wealth, his own comfort, but now he was part of something far greater—a community bound together by love, compassion, and a shared desire to make the world a better place.

As the afternoon turns into evening, the celebration reaches its peak. The musicians play lively tunes, and people dance in the grand ballroom, their laughter ringing out into the night. Children run between the tables, their faces flush with excitement, and Scrooge watches them with a smile, his heart full.

The ballroom is bustling with life. A large clock looms over the room, ticking closer to midnight. Glittering decorations hang from the ceiling, and a band plays cheerful music. The air is filled with laughter, and guests dance and toast in celebration.

Ebenezer Scrooge, dressed in a fine suit, stands at the edge of the crowd, a glass of punch in his hand. He watches the festivities with a soften expression. Fred, his cheerful nephew, is nearby, laughing with his friends. Scrooge smiles faintly, clearly moved by the warmth of the scene. He looks as though he is finally at ease, a man transformed by recent events.

Suddenly, the room seems to hush, as if the air has changed. Scrooge feels it too, a chill running down his spine. He turns, his eyes scanning the room, and then he sees her—BELLE, standing at the entrance, her eyes locked on him. She is older now, her beauty matured but unmistakable, her presence both graceful and commanding.

Scrooge's breath catches in his throat. For a moment, he is transported back in time—to a younger version of himself, to love lost, to the choices that led him here. He blinks, and she is still there, walking towards him, her eyes soft but filled with something unspoken.

"Ebenezer," Belle says softly with a small smile. Scrooge swallows, his eyes wide, his heart pounding. He takes a step forward, his voice barely a whisper.

Belle... is it really you? Scrooge asks. Belle nods, her eyes glistening with emotion. She steps closer, the crowd around them fading into the background, the noise of the celebration muffled as if they are the only two people in the room.

Belle nods, "I heard... I heard about the man you've become. I had to see for myself.

Scrooge looks down, his eyes misty. He takes a deep breath, struggling to find the right words.I... I have changed, Belle. But there hasn't been a day—not a single day—when I haven't thought of you. Of what I lost because of my own foolishness.

Belle's expression softens, a hint of sadness in her eyes. She reaches out, her hand gently touching his arm. "We were young, Ebenezer. We both made choices. But I see now that perhaps... perhaps time has been kinder to us than we realized. Scrooge looks up, his eyes meet hers, filled with hope and regret all at once.

"I don't expect forgiveness. I only wish... I only wish to know if you are happy?"

Belle smiles, a tear escaping down her cheek.

"I have found happiness, Ebenezer. In my own way. And I hope... I hope you find yours too. Scrooge nods, his eyes glistening. He reaches for her hand, and she allows it. They stand there for a moment, two souls reconnecting after years apart, the weight of their past lifting, if only slightly.

"Uncle Scrooge! The countdown!" Fred calls out. The spell breaks. Belle gently pulls her hand away, her eyes still on Scrooge.

"Go, Ebenezer. Enjoy the life you've been given. It's never too late." Scrooge nods, a smile spreading across his face—a real, heartfelt smile. He steps back, his eyes never leaving hers until the crowd swallows him up. Belle watches as he joins Fred, the two of them laughing as the countdown begins.

As Belle walks Scrooge make his way through the crowd, she whispers to herself, "Happy New Year, Ebenezer." The clock strikes midnight. The room erupts in cheers, and Scrooge, amidst the joy and noise, looks back towards the entrance. But Belle is gone, like a memory fading into the night.

Scrooge whispers to himself, "Happy New Year, Belle."

Fireworks explode outside, their colors lighting up the ballroom as Scrooge turns back to Fred, embracing the celebration, a man finally at peace.

As midnight approached, the crowd gathered around the great fir tree, their voices joining together in song. The melody filled the air, a song of hope and joy that seemed to rise up to the very stars above. Scrooge stood among them, his voice joining theirs, his heart light and his spirit soaring.

When the final notes of the song faded into the night, Scrooge looked up at the sky, the stars twinkling above. He thought of the journey he had taken, the changes he had made, and the people who had helped him along the way. He knew that his work was far from over, but he was ready—ready to face each new day with an open heart and a spirit of generosity.

"For the first time in my life," Scrooge whispered to himself, his voice filled with emotion, "That I continue to understand the meaning of Christmas. It is not about wealth or power, but about love, compassion, and the joy of giving."

And as the bells rang out to welcome the New Year, Ebenezer Scrooge stood surrounded by friends, family, and neighbors, his heart filled with hope for the future. He had been given a second chance at life, and he intended to make the most of it—every single day of the year.

Chapter 15

New Beginnings

The New Year brought with it a renewed sense of purpose for Ebenezer Scrooge. The previous night's celebration had filled his heart with hope, and he knew that there was still much work to be done to ensure that his community continued to thrive. Scrooge awoke early, his mind filled with plans for how he could continue to make a difference.

He decided to spend the day visiting the local businesses that had agreed to take on apprentices from the poorhouse. Scrooge wanted to see the apprentices in action, to witness firsthand the difference that opportunity could make in their lives. He bundled himself in his coat and set out, his heart light as he made his way through the snow-covered streets of London.

The first stop on his journey was a blacksmith's shop, where a young man named Thomas had begun his apprenticeship. Scrooge watched from the doorway as Thomas worked alongside the blacksmith, his hands steady as he hammered a glowing piece of metal into shape. The blacksmith, a burly man with a kind smile, nodded approvingly as Thomas completed his task, clapping him on the back in encouragement.

Scrooge stepped inside, his presence drawing the attention of both men. The blacksmith smiled, wiping his hands on his apron as he approached. "Mr. Scrooge! A pleasure to see you. Young Thomas here is doing quite well, I must say."

Thomas looked up, his eyes filled with determination and pride. "Thank you, Mr. Scrooge," he said, his voice earnest. "This is the chance I've always wanted, and I'm going to make the most of it."

Scrooge smiled, his heart swelling with pride. "I have no doubt that you will, Thomas. Keep up the good work, and know that we are all rooting for your success."

After leaving the blacksmith's shop, Scrooge continued his journey, visiting each of the businesses that had taken on apprentices. He saw young men and women learning trades—carpentry, baking, tailoring—each one filled with hope for the future. The business owners spoke highly of their apprentices, praising their dedication and eagerness to learn.

As the day went on, Scrooge found himself filled with a deep sense of fulfillment. He had once been a man who had cared only for his own wealth, but now he saw the true value in investing in others—in giving them the tools they needed to succeed, to build better lives for themselves and their families.

In the afternoon, Scrooge made his way to the poorhouse once more. He wanted to check in on the residents who had not yet begun their apprenticeships, to see how they were faring. The overseer greeted him at the door, his expression softer than it had been during Scrooge's previous visits.

"Mr. Scrooge," the overseer said, his voice respectful, "the changes you have brought to this place... they have made a world of difference. The people here have hope now, and that is something they have not had in a very long time."

Scrooge nodded, his eyes misting over as he looked around the room. The residents were gathered in small groups, talking and laughing, their faces filled with a sense of purpose. He approached a young mother, her child playing at her feet, and knelt down to speak with her.

"How are you, my dear?" Scrooge asked, his voice gentle.

The young mother looked up, her eyes filled with gratitude. "We are well, Mr. Scrooge. Thanks to you, we have hope again. My son will grow up with opportunities that I never had, and for that, I will be forever grateful."

Scrooge smiled, his heart swelling with emotion. "You are most welcome, my dear. And remember, this is only the beginning. There are many more opportunities ahead for you and your son."

Before leaving the poorhouse, Scrooge gathered the residents for a brief meeting. He wanted to make sure that each one of them knew they were not forgotten and that there were opportunities waiting for them. He spoke to them about the apprenticeships that were still available, and he promised to personally help them find their paths forward. The faces of the residents lit up with renewed hope, and Scrooge knew that his work here was far from finished.

As the sun began to set, Scrooge made his way back home, his heart filled with a sense of peace. He had seen the impact of his actions, the difference that hope and opportunity could make in the lives of others. He knew that his journey was far from over, but he was ready—ready to face each new day with an open heart and a spirit of generosity.

"For the first time in my life," Scrooge whispered to himself as he walked through the quiet streets, "I truly understand the meaning of a second chance. It is not just about changing oneself—it is about lifting others up, about giving them the chance to build a better future."

And as he reached his doorstep, Scrooge paused, looking up at the night sky, the stars twinkling above. He thought of his beloved sister, Fan, and all that she had meant to him. He remembered the promise he had made to honor her memory and to live a life that she would be proud of. Tears welled in his eyes, but they were tears of joy, for he knew that he was finally on the right path.

"For you, dear Fan," he whispered, his voice full of love and resolve. "For you, and for everyone who deserves a second chance."

And with that, Ebenezer Scrooge stepped inside his home, his heart brimming with hope and determination. He knew that the spirit of Christmas would guide him every day, and he vowed to make each day a testament to love, compassion, and the joy of giving. He dresses for bed but opts to sit in his favorite armchair and enjoy the fire and a small cup of tea. He places the cup on the side table and opens the box containing the locket. He looks at the picture of Fan, and falls asleep.

As he sleeps, in his dream, he hears the faint sound of children's laughter echoes faintly, growing louder as the shadows ripple across the room. The locket in Scrooge's hand begins to glow faintly. He looks up, startled, as the shadows coalesce into a shimmering doorway.

"What is this now?" he asks. A child's voice calls out from beyond the doorway.

"Ebenezer!" Scrooge rises, gripping the locket tightly as he steps forward.

Scrooge finds himself in a cold, austere schoolroom. The benches are empty save for him as a child, no more than ten years old, sitting hunched over a battered book. Snow drifts in through the cracks in the windows. A door creaks open, and Fan bursts in, her cheeks flushed with excitement.

"Ebenezer! Father's sent for you! The young Scrooge looks up, his face pale and weary.

"Home? Truly?" he asks. Fan rushes to his side, pulling him to his feet.

"Yes! He's changed! It'll be Christmas, just like it used to be."

Young Scrooge hesitates, then smiles shyly, allowing her to drag him toward the door. The scene freezes as the adult Scrooge steps forward, watching the memory with a bittersweet expression.

"Fan... you were always my light in the dark." The shadows twist again, and the memory shifts. Scrooge continues to toss and turn in his armchair, not comprehending what was in store.

He now finds himself standing in a dimly lit bedroom. Fan lies on a narrow bed, her face pale and drawn. He sees himself standing at the foot of the bed, his posture stiff.

"Stay with me, Ebenezer. Just a little longer." Young Scrooge hesitates, glancing at the door.

"But there is much to be done at the office, Fan. I'll return shortly." Fan's eyes glisten with disappointment as he leaves. The memory shifts again, showing Scrooge returning to find the bed empty, the room eerily quiet. The dream ends abruptly, and Scrooge straightens in his armchair, his breathing shallow. He clutches the locket to his chest.

"I should have stayed. I should have been there," Scrooge whispers. The shadows ripple again, but this time they take the form of a familiar figure. Marley appears, his chains clinking faintly.

"Is this truly you, Marley?" Scrooge asks.

"Fan never blamed you, Ebenezer. But you've carried her loss like another chain," Marley replies. Scrooge turns, his eyes wide.

"Marley. You've returned." Marley steps closer, his expression grave.

"I'm here Ebenezer, to remind you that redemption is not simply a matter of intent. It requires action."

"I understand that Jacob. I truly do. I am trying, Jacob. I swear it. Marley nods slowly.

"Then do not falter. For others still bear the weight of your past." Marley begins to fade, the sound of his chains fading with him.

"No, Wait! Jacob, wait!" The room falls silent, leaving Scrooge alone with his thoughts.

Chapter 16

A Heartfelt Goodbye

The day after New Year's, Ebenezer Scrooge found himself in his office, reviewing the ledgers alongside Bob Cratchit and his eldest son, Peter. The office was warm, the fireplace crackling with a gentle glow that filled the room. Bob and Peter worked diligently, and there was a sense of ease and contentment that had not existed in the old office before.

Scrooge looked up from his work, his eyes softening as he observed Bob and his son. He felt a warmth in his heart that came from knowing that his newfound generosity had made life better for the Cratchits. After all those years of demanding work and meager pay, Bob was now receiving the respect and compensation he deserved, and Peter had a future that was bright and full of promise.

"Well, Bob, Peter," Scrooge said, closing the ledger in front of him, "I think that's enough work for today. You two should head home and spend the rest of the day with your family. By the way Peter. You are becoming an outstanding clerk."

Bob looked up, a smile spreading across his face. "Thank you, Mr. Scrooge. You've been more than kind to us. We're truly grateful."

Peter nodded eagerly. "Yes, sir. Thank you for everything."

Scrooge waved his hand dismissively, though a smile played on his lips. "Think nothing of it, my boy. Family is what truly matters. Now, off you go. I'll lock up here."

Bob and Peter gathered their things, and after exchanging warm farewells, they left the office. Scrooge watched them go, his heart swelling with pride and affection. He donned his coat and hat, preparing to leave for the evening as well.

Stepping out into the crisp evening air, Scrooge took a deep breath, savoring the quiet of the town as he made his way through the cobbled streets. The gas lamps flickered, casting a warm glow on the snow-covered ground. It was a peaceful night, and Scrooge felt a profound sense of contentment.

As he approached the town square, he suddenly heard a shout from behind him. "Uncle Scrooge! Uncle Scrooge!"

Scrooge turned, his eyes widening as he saw a small figure running towards him. It was Tiny Tim, his little legs moving as fast as they could carry him, his face beaming with excitement.

"Tim, my boy!" Scrooge called out, his heart leaping with joy. He knelt down just in time for Tim to throw himself into Scrooge's arms, wrapping his small arms around the old man's neck.

Scrooge held Tim close, his eyes misting over as he felt the boy's warmth against him. "What are you doing out here, lad?" he asked gently, pulling back to look at Tim's smiling face.

"Mama said I could come and say goodnight properly," Tim replied, his eyes shining with happiness. "I wanted to thank you again, Uncle. For everything you've done for us. And… and I wanted to tell you that I love you."

Scrooge felt his throat tighten, and he blinked back tears. He cupped Tim's cheek, his voice thick with emotion. "And I love you too, Tim. More than words can say. You've brought so much joy into my life, my dear boy."

Tim beamed, his smile lighting up the night. "Papa says you're like part of our family now. And I think so too."

Scrooge's heart swelled with love, and he nodded, his voice barely a whisper. "That means more to me than you'll ever know, Tim. Now, let's get you back to your father before he starts to worry."

Scrooge stood, lifting Tim into his arms, and they began walking together through the softly falling snow. As they walked, Tim rested his head against Scrooge's shoulder, his small hand clutching the collar of Scrooge's coat.

The town square was quiet, the decorations from the previous night's celebration still hanging, swaying gently in the breeze. Scrooge looked up at the fir tree in the center of the square, its candles now extinguished but still beautiful in the moonlight. He felt a deep sense of peace, knowing that he was no longer alone—that he was part of something greater than himself.

"Uncle," Tim said softly, his voice breaking the silence. "Do you think we'll always be this happy?"

Scrooge smiled, his eyes fixed on the stars above. "I believe we will, Tim. As long as we have each other, and as long as we carry the spirit of Christmas in our hearts, we will always find joy and happiness."

Tim lifted his head, looking up at Scrooge with wide eyes. "Promise?"

Scrooge looked down at the boy, his eyes filled with love. "I promise, my dear boy. I promise."

As they continued their walk, the bells of the town church began to chime, signaling the late hour. Scrooge paused, listening to the gentle ringing, letting it wash over him like a soothing lullaby. Each chime was a reminder of time's passage, a symbol of the new life he had embraced. He turned his gaze back to Tim, whose face was filled with wonder at the sound of the bells.

"You know, Tim," Scrooge said, his voice thoughtful, "those bells remind me of how precious every moment is. Every day is a gift, and it's up to us to make the most of it. That's what I've learned, and that's what I want for you—to live each day with joy, kindness, and courage."

Tim nodded slowly, his eyes filled with admiration for the old man. "I will, Uncle. I promise I'll make every day count."

Scrooge smiled, his heart swelling with pride. "That's all I could ever ask for, lad."

They continued walking, the snowflakes drifting down around them, blanketing the town in a soft, quiet beauty. The streets were empty, the world at peace, and Scrooge felt a sense of completeness that he had never known before. He thought of his sister, Fan, and imagined her looking down on him with pride. He thought of the past, of the mistakes he had made, and of the future that lay ahead—bright and full of promise.

As they reached the Cratchit home, Scrooge gently set Tim down on the doorstep. He knelt to look Tim in the eye, his own eyes filled with warmth. "Now, off to bed with you, young man. And remember—no matter what happens, you are never alone. You have your family, and you have me."

Tim threw his arms around Scrooge once more, hugging him tightly. "Goodnight, Uncle. I love you."

Scrooge held the boy close, his voice a whisper. "Goodnight, Tim. And may God bless us, everyone."

With a final wave, Tim slipped inside the house, and Scrooge stood there for a moment, watching the door close. He turned and began his walk home, his heart full. The town was silent, the only sound the crunch of his boots on the snow. He walked slowly, savoring the peace of the night, knowing that he was exactly where he was meant to be.

As he reached his own doorstep, Scrooge looked up at the sky, the stars twinkling brightly above. He took a deep breath, feeling the cold air fill his lungs, and he smiled. He had been given a second chance, and he intended to make every moment count.

"For you, dear Fan," he whispered to the night sky, "and for everyone who believes in the power of love and redemption."

And with that, Ebenezer Scrooge stepped inside his home, the warmth of the fire greeting him as he closed the door behind him. He knew that the spirit of Christmas would live in his heart every day, guiding him to be the man he had always been meant to be—a man of love, of compassion, and of endless hope.

I hope you've enjoyed my story about the life of Ebenezer Scrooge after his famous Christmas transformation. To add to the wonder of this timeless tale, here are some fascinating facts about Charles Dickens' classic *A Christmas Carol*:

Dickens penned the novella in just six weeks, spurred by financial pressures. It's said he found inspiration during hour-long nighttime walks through the streets of London.

First published on December 19, 1843, *A Christmas Carol* became an instant sensation, with the first edition selling out by Christmas Eve. Over nearly two centuries, the story has remained a beloved holiday staple, inspiring countless stage and screen adaptations. Its immediate success was so overwhelming that just a month after its debut, Dickens found himself in a legal battle against a publisher of pirated copies. By 1844, the novella had gone through 13 printings and remains a bestseller more than 175 years later.

Despite its popularity, Dickens didn't make much money from early editions of the book. His meticulous attention to detail—such as the endpapers and binding—cut deeply into his profits.

Interestingly, *A Christmas Carol* was just one of several Christmas-themed stories Dickens wrote. The full title of the novella is *A Christmas Carol. In Prose. Being a Ghost Story of Christmas.*

Like many of his works, it was a piece of social commentary, reflecting Dickens' deep commitment to helping the underserved. His own experience with poverty—his family's imprisonment in a debtors' prison forced him to leave school as a boy and work in a factory—inspired him to write stories that shed light on the struggles of the poor.

As Dickens' biographer Michael Slater noted, Dickens saw *A Christmas Carol* as a way to "help open the hearts of the prosperous and powerful towards the poor and powerless."

Dickens personally revised his original 66-page manuscript and had it bound in crimson leather with gilt decorations before gifting it to his friend and creditor, Thomas Mitton. Today, a digital copy of the manuscript is available through the Morgan Library & Museum.

Over the years, *A Christmas Carol* has inspired more than 100 adaptations, including a 1908 short film starring Tom Ricketts—an actor who reportedly directed the first movie ever made in Hollywood—and the 2015 TV movie *A Christmas Carol and Zombies*. The story has also been featured in over 20 TV shows, including *Sanford and Son, Family Ties, DuckTales,* and *The Jetsons*.

Additionally, there are two ballet adaptations and four operas based on the novella, including *The Passion of Scrooge*, a chamber opera for one baritone and orchestra.

Although the novella was widely praised by Dickens' peers, it didn't resonate with everyone. A 32-year-old Mark Twain, for example, dismissed it as "nothing but glittering frostwork, with no heart or feeling."

With all that said, *A Christmas Carol: The Next Chapter* is the first novel to revisit the world of Ebenezer Scrooge, continuing his story the day after his profound transformation.

www.ingramcontent.com/pod-product-compliance
Lightning Source LLC
Chambersburg PA
CBHW040235110526
44582CB00020B/202/J